OLD
TESTAMENT
EXEGESIS

OLD
TESTAMENT
EXEGESIS

THIRD EDITION

A HANDBOOK FOR
STUDENTS AND PASTORS

DOUGLAS STUART

WJK WESTMINSTER
JOHN KNOX PRESS
LOUISVILLE · KENTUCKY

Book design by Sharon Adams
Cover design by Mark Abrams

Third edition

Published by Westminster John Knox Press
Louisville, Kentucky

This book is printed on acid-free paper that meets the American National Standards Institute Z39.48 standard. ∞

PRINTED IN THE UNITED STATES OF AMERICA

06 07 08 09 — 10 9 8 7 6

Library of Congress Cataloging in Publication Data

Stuart, Douglas
    Old Testament exegesis: a handbook for students and pastors
    / Douglas Stuart.—3rd ed.
        p. cm.
    Includes bibliographical references.
    ISBN-13: 978-0-664-22315-1 (alk. paper)
    ISBN-10: 0-664-22315-X (alk. paper)
        1. Bibl. O.T.—Hermeneutics. 2. Bible. O.T.—Homiletical use.
    3. Bible. O.T.—Bibliography. I. Title.

BS476 .S83 2001
221.6'01—dc21   2001035510

To
Gayle, Joanna, Eliza, Eden, Missy,
Hannah, Maria, Delia, and Jon

CONTENTS

Abbreviations

BH3	*Biblia Hebraica*, 3d ed. (Stuttgart: Württembergische Bibelanstalt, 1937)
BHS	*Biblia Hebraica Stuttgartensia* (Stuttgart: Deutsche Bibelstiftung, 1977)
LXX	The Septuagint
MT	The Masoretic Text
NT	New Testament
OT	Old Testament

Preface

THOSE FEW STUDENTS AND PASTORS who control several ancient and modern languages, read the scholarly literature regularly, and have already gained some confidence of their ability to do exegesis will certainly not need this primer. It is written for those who cannot read a Hebrew psalm at sight and who are not sure what *Vetus Testamentum* would mean or contain (the words mean "Old Testament" in Latin, and are the title of a major OT scholarly journal). It is for those who have no idea what *homoioteleuton* might be (this term means "same kind of ending" and is a factor in certain textual problems). It is for the vast majority of all seminary students and pastors. It is predicated on the conviction that even the most intelligent people cannot understand procedures and concepts that are not somehow explained to them, and that there is no shame in seeking such explanations in spite of the fact that most seminary professors do not volunteer them. Old Testament exegesis has regular procedures and concepts, and these can be taught to almost anyone willing to learn. It is a tragedy that so few seminary students ever really feel sure of themselves in doing OT exegesis—and most pastors apparently abandon the practice altogether.

I have set out, therefore, to present a step-by-step guide to OT exegesis that will be nontechnical and simple without being simplistic, that will explain not only the procedures but the goals of exegesis, and that will serve as a handbook for reference as the student or pastor does the actual work of exegesis.

My approach to exegesis has certain conscious biases for which I make no apologies. Perhaps the most debatable is my insistence that exegesis should include guidelines for application of the passage being studied. Exegesis is patently a theological enterprise, and a theology that is not applied to the lives of God's people is sterile. For this reason, too, I have purposely de-emphasized some of the critical techniques (e.g., structuralism, redaction criticism) which, though fascinating to the scholar, yield meager rewards theologically and are, in the final analysis, of minor value homiletically, much as that value judgment may displease some scholars. I have tried to set a fair balance between synchronic and diachronic techniques (i.e., techniques concerned respectively with the text as it stands, and with the history of the developments that led to the text as it stands), but only insofar as these, too, hold promise of practical, theological benefit. The end of exegesis is preaching and teaching in the church. Seminary students and pastors know this instinctively and demand relevance from exegesis and other biblical studies, as well they should.

This primer recognizes that very few American students and pastors can read German or other scholarly languages. Of what advantage, therefore, is it to pretend that they can? The bibliographical guidance in chapter 4 is thus restricted as much as possible to English works.

A unique feature of this book is found in chapter 3, which outlines an abbreviated, limited-time exegetical format for pastors. Seminary students usually learn at least in a general way how to produce formal exegesis term papers, based on dozens of hours of research and writing. But no one tells them how they can transfer that ability to the weekly preaching task, where perhaps only four or five hours may be available for the exegesis part of the sermon preparation. Exegesis can be done responsibly even if not exhaustively in a few hours' time. The pastor should first try to understand the fuller form of the guide in chapter 1. Chapter 3 represents a condensation and economization of the same material, with special attention paid to homiletical interests.

Those aspiring OT exegetes who know no Hebrew should still be able to make good use of the guidance given here—but there can be no denying that at least some knowledge of Hebrew is a precious advantage for student and pastor alike. I have done everything possible to encourage those whose Hebrew is weak to use it anyway. The helps discussed in chapter 4 can go a long way toward overcoming the disadvantages, especially via computer concordances that can instantly provide a range of Hebrew-English resources once found only at great effort. Indeed, the pastor who faithfully works from the biblical languages in sermon preparation, no matter how rusty his or her knowledge of them may be at the start, can't help gaining a fair language mastery as time goes by. I hope this primer will encourage many to try.

For the third edition I have added some new explanations, added or deleted or altered hundreds of sentences, included scores of additional reference works, updated the listings of works that have been revised, and tried to provide other improvements throughout as well. Thus this edition is revised and expanded substantially. I am very grateful to my students Wendy Wilcox Glidden and Filip Vukosavovic for dozens of suggestions that have been incorporated into this latest edition. It is a joy to work with students who love books and learning and want others to share their delight.

The widespread use of the first and second editions, including their foreign language translations, has been very gratifying and is evidence of an ongoing hunger for preaching and teaching based accurately and confidently in the Scriptures.

ANALYTICAL
TABLE OF CONTENTS

(FOR CROSS-REFERENCE USE)

Chapter 2. **Exegesis and the Original Text**

Chapter 3. **Short Guide for Sermon Exegesis**

Chapter 4. **Exegesis Aids and Resources**

INTRODUCTION

A N EXEGESIS IS A THOROUGH, analytical study of a biblical passage
done so as to arrive at a useful interpretation of the passage. Exegesis is a theological task, but not a mystical one. There are certain basic rules and standards for how to do it, although the results
can vary in appearance because the biblical passages themselves vary
so much.

To do OT exegesis properly, you have to be something of a gener-
alist. You will quickly become involved with the functions and meanings of words (linguistics); the analysis of literature and speech
(philology); theology; history; the transmission of the biblical writings (textual criticism); stylistics, grammar, and vocabulary analysis;
and the vaguely defined yet inescapably important area of sociology.
Natural intuitive skills are helpful but no substitute for the hard work
of careful, firsthand research. Exegesis as a process can be quite dull.
Its results, fortunately, can often be exciting. Exciting or not, the
results should always at least be of genuine practical value to the
believer or something is wrong with the exegesis. While this book is
a primer, and hardly an exhaustive analysis of exegetical presuppositions or techniques, it ought to serve you well if your reason for
learning exegesis is eventually to apply its benefits in Christian
preaching or teaching.

An exegete must work from many books and sources. Four kinds are especially valuable for the methodological and bibliographical guidance they contain relating to exegesis. You should own all four kinds, of which the following are representative samples:

> Raymond Dillard and Tremper Longman, *An Introduction to the Old Testament* (Zondervan Publishing House, 1994)

or

> J. Alberto Soggin, *Introduction to the Old Testament*, rev. ed. (Westminster John Knox Press, 1999)

Both of these introductions contain lucid, concrete explanations of OT literary types and divisions, scholarly approaches, book-by-book content and criticism, canon and text. Moreover, there is much to be gained from either book's bibliographical guidance.

> Frederick W. Danker, *Multipurpose Tools for Bible Study*, rev. ed. (Fortress Press, 1993)

Danker provides backgrounds, definitions, and explanations for all sorts of books, methods, sources, and styles in biblical exegesis. His work is a standard resource for such information.

> Richard N. Soulen, *Handbook of Biblical Criticism*, rev. and aug'd ed. (John Knox Press, 1985)

The *Handbook* is a collection of definitions. Virtually all the exegetical terms and techniques you'll run across are explained in full by Soulen.

> Joseph A. Fitzmyer, *An Introductory Bibliography for the Study of Scripture*, 3d ed. (Loyola Press, 1990)

Fitzmyer's *Bibliography* is one of the best annotated listings (through its publication date) of lexicons, texts, grammars, concordances, and other technical aids used by exegetes.

With these four kinds of texts in hand, you'll know what the issues in exegesis are, what kind of resources are available, and where to find them.

In addition to these four sorts of books, you ought to have in your library a copy of the Hebrew OT, a Hebrew-based concordance, a Hebrew lexicon, a Hebrew grammar, a comprehensive history of Israel, a Bible dictionary, and a "critical" commentary series (if possible). The specific works are discussed in chapter 4. The concordance, history, dictionary, and commentary series are essential even if you don't know Hebrew. Without the proper tools, an exegesis can't go very far. Of course, the more of these sorts of works you have via computer software, the faster your exegesis work will go.

Remember as you use this guide that all the steps do not apply equally to all OT passages. For example, some passages will require major attention to historical issues and very little attention to their form or vocabulary; others will be just the opposite. There is no way to be sure of this automatically in advance. As you become familiar with a passage it will tend to become obvious to you how to assign the relative weight of each step, and the subpoints thereof.

This primer is organized into four sections. Chapter 1 provides a nontechnical format for term papers and other full, formal exegesis projects. Chapter 2 gives illustrations for the steps of a full exegesis. Chapter 3 gives a simple, condensed version of the longer format, which centers especially on sermon preparation. Chapter 4 discusses the various exegetical aids and resources, especially bibliographical, and how to use them.

I

Guide for Full Exegesis

THE OUTLINE IS SUPPLEMENTED WITH large numbers of comments and questions intended to help you leave no stone unturned in doing a thorough exegesis. It is important to note that these comments and questions are primarily suggestive and not to be followed slavishly. Indeed, some questions overlap and some may seem redundant to you. Some may not be relevant to your purposes or the scope of your particular exegesis needs in any given passage. So be selective. Ignore what does not apply to your passage and task. Emphasize what does.

Pastors and others who will work mainly from the guide for sermon exegesis in chapter 3 should familiarize themselves with the content of this chapter first, as it constitutes the basis for the condensation in chapter 3.

1. Text

1.1. Confirm the limits of the passage.

Try to be sure that the passage you have chosen for exegesis is a genuine, self-contained unit (sometimes called a pericope). Avoid cutting a poem in the middle of a stanza, or a narrative in the middle of a paragraph—unless that is the assignment you are working under, or unless you explain clearly to your reader why you have chosen to exegete a *section* of a full passage. Your primary ally is common sense. Does your passage have a recognizable beginning and end? Does it have some sort of cohesive, meaningful content that you can observe? Check your decision against both the Hebrew text and modern translations. Do not trust the chapter and verse divisions. They are not original and are often completely misleading.

Note: You may find it confusing to begin with the textual analysis of your passage if your knowledge of Hebrew is not yet adequate. In that case, first prepare a rough, even wooden translation of the passage from the Hebrew. Do not delay yourself needlessly at this point. Use a trustworthy modern translation as your guide, or an interlinear if you wish (see 4.2.2). Once you have a working idea of what the Hebrew words mean, you can resume the textual analysis with profit.

1.2. Compare the versions.

From as many as you can read of the Greek, Syriac, Aramaic, Latin, and Qumran versions of the passage, isolate any words or phrases that do not seem to correspond to the Hebrew text you are working on. Since all of these ancient language versions have English translations (see 4.2.2), you can actually work from them preliminarily even if you do not know one or more of these languages.

Refer to the critical apparatus in the *BHS* (or apparatuses in the older *BH3* if you are using it), even though it is not always complete and can be difficult to decipher because it is written in abbreviated Latin (for deciphering, the guides in 4.1.5 are very helpful). Examine the differences (called variants). Try to decide, as best you can, whether any of the variants are possibly more appropriate to the passage (i.e., possibly more original) than the corresponding words in the Hebrew text. To do this, you must translate the variant back into Hebrew (normally via English) and then judge whether it fits the context better. Very often you can see exactly how a variant came to result from a corruption (an ancient copying mistake that became preserved in the subsequent copies) in the Hebrew text. Make these decisions as best you can, referring to critical commentaries and other aids (see 4.1). All too often, especially in a poetic section, a corruption will be insoluble: the wording may not make much sense in the Hebrew as it stands, but you cannot figure out a convincing alternative. In such cases, leave the received text alone. Your task is to reconstruct *as far as possible* the text as originally inspired by God, not to rewrite it.

1.3. Reconstruct and annotate the text.

Put on paper for your reader your best guess at the original Hebrew text. Print out the reconstructed original text in full. If your reconstruction omits any words or letters from the received text, mark the omissions by square brackets: [ ]. If you insert or replace any words or letters, place the new part inside angle brackets: < >. Mark each such spot with a raised letter or number (letters are best since they can't be confused with verse numbers) and in the footnotes explain clearly and simply your reasons for the changes. It is advisable also to footnote any words you did not change but which someone else might think ought to be changed. Your reader deserves an explanation of all your significant decisions for or against changes in the text, not just those that result in actual changes.

Normally, this reconstructed text should constitute the beginning of your exegesis paper, following immediately upon the preface (if any), table of contents (if any), and introduction. Textual problems are rarely so frequent or major as to affect the sense of a passage. The rare proposed textual revision (from the MT) that materially affects the sense of the passage will probably require a major digression at this point in the paper.

1.4. Present poetry in versified form.

In most cases you can trust the *BHS* (or *BH3*) to identify poetry properly and to arrange the lines of poetry according to the *BHS* editor's sense of parallelism and rhythm (meter). The process of arrangement and the arrangement itself are both referred to as stichometry.

The parallelism between the words and phrases is the main criterion for deciding the stichometry. A secondary criterion is the meter (see 4.6.4). If you decide on a different stichometry for your passage from the one indicated by *BH3* or *BHS* (their stichometries are not always right), be sure to give the reader your reasoning in a footnote. The modern English translations usually arrange poetry stichometrically. Consult them as well, because their sense of how the parallelism works can be both instructive and timesaving.

2. Translation

2.1. Prepare a tentative translation of your reconstructed tex.

Start fresh, from the beginning. Look up in a lexicon such as Holladay's (see 4.8.1) all words whose range of meaning you are not absolutely certain of. For the more significant words, try at least to skim the more lengthy lexicon articles in major lexicons such as Koehler-Baumgartner or Brown-Driver-Briggs (see 4.8.1). For any words that appear to be central or pivotal for the meaning of your passage, it is advisable either at this point or in connection with your analysis of the lexical content (step 8.3) to consult the detailed word studies (concept studies) in the aids referred to in 4.8.3. Remember that most words don't have a single meaning, but rather a range of meaning(s), and that there is a difference between a word and a concept (at 8.3 we explain this further). A single Hebrew word rarely corresponds precisely to a single English word but may range in meaning through all or parts of several different English words. Translation therefore always involves selection.

2.2. Check the correspondence of text and translation.

Read your Hebrew text over and over. Know it as a friend. Memorize parts of it if possible. Read your translation over and over (out loud). Do the Hebrew and your English seem the same in your mind? Have you used a rare or complicated English word to translate a common or simple Hebrew word? If so, does the resulting precision of meaning outweigh in value the disruptive effect on the reader or hearer? Have you considered the possibility of using several English words to convey the meaning of one Hebrew word? Or vice versa? Does your passage contain words or phrases that originally were genuinely ambiguous? If so, try to reproduce rather than mask the ambiguity in your English translation. A good translation is one that creates the same general impression for the hearer as the original would, without distorting the particular content conveyed.

2.3. Revise the translation as you continue.

As you continue to exegete your passage, especially as you examine carefully the grammatical and lexical data, you will almost certainly learn enough to make improvements in your tentative translation. This is because the word(s) you choose for a given spot in the passage need to fit the overall context well. The more you know about the whole passage, the better you will have a proper "feel" for selecting the right word, phrase or expression in each part. The part should fit the whole. Also, as you make decisions about the literary and theological contexts of your passage, you will likewise be developing better judgment about the translation. Try to evaluate the use of a word, phrase, or expression both in its broad contexts (the book, the OT, the Bible as a whole) and its immediate contexts (your passage, the chapter, the surrounding chapters). The difference can be significant. For example, although you might have assumed that the Hebrew word בַּיִת means "house" in your passage, a wider look at its uses throughout the OT shows that in an expression like בֵּית דָּוִיד it can mean "family," "dynasty," or "lineage." Which suits your passage better? Which makes your passage clearer to the reader? By asking these questions, you help guarantee that you will not overlook potentially useful translation options.

2.4. Provide a finished translation.

After your research is complete and you are ready to write the final draft, place the finished translation immediately following the text. Use annotations (footnotes—again, letters are less likely to cause confusion with verse numbers than numbers are) to explain choices of wording that might be surprising or simply not obvious to your reader. You are not obliged, however, to explain any word that was also chosen by several modern versions, unless it seems to you that their choice, even if unanimous, is questionable in some way. Use the footnotes to tell the reader other possible translations of a word or phrase that you consider to have merit. Do this especially wherever you find it difficult to choose between two or more options.

3. Historical Context

3.1. Research the historical background.

Try to answer the following questions in your research: What is the setting of the passage? Exactly what events led up to this point? Did major trends or developments in Israel or the rest of the ancient world have any bearing on the passage or any part of its content? Are there any parallel or similar passages in the Bible that seem to be related to the same historical conditions? If so, do they provide any insight into your passage? Under what historical conditions does the passage seem to have been written? Might the passage have been written also under very different historical conditions? If not, why not? Does the passage bring to an end or represent some particular stage in the progress of any events or concepts? From this point and onward, take note of how the information you have learned about your passage has an effect on its interpretation. Explain how this historical information helps one to understand or appreciate the passage in some way. Be sure to exploit any archaeological data that may exist concerning the passage. In some instances it may not be possible to determine anything specific about the historical background of your passage. For example, this is sometimes the case with poetic passages, such as psalms or proverbs intended to be meaningful at all times and places. If so, explain this to the reader. Describe the implications of the lack of a clear historical context, if any, for your passage.

3.2. Research the social setting.

Try to answer the following questions: Where in Israel's life are the content or events of the passage located? What social and civil institutions bear upon the passage? How do they illumine the passage? Is the passage or some portion of it directly relevant only to an ancient Israelite (i.e., culturally "bound") or is it useful and meaningful today, and to what extent? Over what range of time or what breadth of Israelite (or other) culture would events of the passage (or its concepts) have been possible or likely? Are the events or concepts uniquely Israelite, or could they have occurred or been expressed elsewhere?

3.3. Research the historical foreground.

What comes next? What does the passage lead to? What that is significant ultimately happens to the people, places, things, and concepts of the passage? Does the passage contain information that is essential to understanding something else that occurs or is said later? Is the passage at the start of any new developments? Where does the passage fit in the general scope of OT history? Are there any implications that follow from its placement?

3.4. Research the geographical setting.

Does the passage have a provenience (a geographical setting or "origin")? In which nation, region, tribal territory, or village do the events or concepts of the passage apply? Is it, for example, a northern or southern passage (i.e., either reflecting a northern or southern origin, or else focusing especially on northern or southern kingdom matters), or an intra-Israel or extra-Israel passage, or is that impossible to discern? Does it have a national or regional perspective? Is it localized in any way? Do issues such as climate, topography, ethnic distribution, regional culture, or economy play a role? Is there anything else about the nature of the geography that illuminates the passage's content in some way?

3.5. Date the passage.

If the passage is a historical narrative, seek the date for the events as described. If it is a prophetic oracle (revealed message), seek the date when it might have been delivered by the prophet. If it is poetry of some other sort, try to determine when it might have been composed.

Arriving at a precise date is not always possible. Be especially cautious in using secondary literature, since a scholar's critical methodology largely determines to what extent he or she will tend to consider portions of the Bible as "authentic"—genuinely representative of the time and events of which they speak, or not "authentic"—actually products of a later historical period—and date them accordingly.

If you cannot suggest a specific date, at least suggest the date before which the passage could not have occurred or been composed (called the *terminus a quo*) and the date by which the passage surely must have already taken place or been composed (called the *terminus ad quem*). The context and content of the passage, including its vocabulary, are your main guides to date.

Dating prophetic passages precisely is often difficult or impossible. In most cases the only way to proceed is to try to link the message of the passage with historical circumstances known from OT historical portions and other ancient Near Eastern historical sources. This is typically what the commentaries do in such cases. Sometimes it is possible to identify a historical circumstance that forms the background for or subject of an oracle. Many times it is not, and the oracle can be dated no more precisely than within the limits of the book as a whole.

4. Literary Context

Some overlap is bound to exist between the historical context and the literary context. The Old Testament is a historically oriented revelation, and therefore its literary progressions and orderings will tend to correspond to the actual history of Yahweh's dealings with his people.

4.1. Examine the literary function.

Is your passage part of a story or a literary grouping that has a discernible beginning, middle, and end? Does it fill in, add on, introduce, bring to completion, or counterbalance the book or section of a book of which it is a part? Is it self-contained? Could it be placed elsewhere, or is it essential to its present context? What does it add to the overall picture? What does the overall picture add to it?

4.2. Examine the placement.

Just how does it fit within the section, book, division, Testament, Bible—in that order? What can you discover about its style, type, purpose, degree of literary integration (degree to which the passage is linked or "woven into" the rest of the book), literary function, etc.? Is it one of many similar texts in the same book, or perhaps in the OT as a whole? In what sense is its nature unique to the surrounding material, and/or its position within that material somehow unique?

4.3. Analyze the detail.

How comprehensive is the passage? If it is historical, how selective has it been? What things does it concentrate on, and what does it leave unsaid? Does it report the events from a special perspective? If so, what does that tell you about the special purpose of the passage? How does its perspective relate to the larger context? If it is poetic, how narrow or broad is its range? Do any details help you decide whether it was written in connection with a specific cultural or historical situation? Do any details give you insight into the author's intentions?

4.4. Analyze the authorship.

Is the author of the passage identified or identifiable? If the author can be identified, how certain is the identification? If the passage is anonymous, is it possible to suggest generally the probable human source or milieu out of which God communicated his word? Can the time of its composition be discerned, whether or not the identity of the author can be known for sure? Is it possible that material originally written by someone else has been reused, adapted, or incorporated into a larger structure by a later inspired "writer" or "editor"? Does this tell you anything theologically? Does it help you follow the logic of the passage better? If the author is known either explicitly or implicitly, does this knowledge help you connect the passage, including its motifs, style, vocabulary, etc., with other portions of Scripture from the hand of the same author? Is this in any way instructive for the interpretation of the passage? Does the author here reveal any unique features (stylistically, for example), or is the passage typical of his or her writing elsewhere?

5. Form

5.1. Identify the general literary type (genre).

First locate the passage within the broad, general categories of literary types contained in the OT. Decide whether your passage is a prose type, a saying, a "song," or a combination (such basic categories are defined in any of the general guides to form analysis listed in 4.1.2).

5.2. Identify the specific literary type (form).

Describe more precisely what sort of prose type, saying, or song the passage actually is. For example, if you decide that it is a historical narrative, you must then go on to judge whether it is a report, a popular history, a general autobiography, a dream-vision account, a prophetic autobiography, or some other specific kind of historical narrative. Identifying the specific type is what allows you to compare it to other such types and thus learn what elements in your passage are typical of its literary form and what elements are unique and thus of special value for interpreting your passage as opposed to others.

You must know both the general and the specific literary type of your passage before you are in a position to analyze its form or forms. Only the specific—not the general—types have "forms." That is, every specific literary type is identifiable because it has certain recognizable features (including both its contents or "ingredients" and the order in which those ingredients occur) that make it a form. For example, each "dream account" in the OT tends to have certain features that it shares with all the other dream accounts. The specific contents of the various dream accounts may be different, but the features are not; each dream account contains roughly the same sorts of things. They are said to have the same form, which we call the "dream account form."

5.3. Look for subcategories.

A main purpose of form analysis is to compare your passage with others of like form and to exploit the knowledge that results from that comparison. It is therefore best to describe a form as specifically as possible without making it unique. For example, if your passage contained a dream account that included a conversation between an angel and a prophet, you would probably gain more fruitful exegetical data from a comparison of your dream account with those others which also contain a prophet-angel dialogue, rather than with all dream accounts in general. You might even decide that tentatively you will call your form a "prophet-angel dialogue dream account." As you will soon notice if you are not already aware of it, the terminology used by scholars in form analysis is not very standardized—certainly not so standardized as to rule out a certain cautiously exercised freedom of terminology on your part. However, do not try to subcategorize your form to the extent that it becomes one of a kind. At that point it is meaningless even to speak of a form, and the crucial benefits of comparison are lost. Those elements which cannot be compared are the special elements that call for careful attention elsewhere in your exe-

gesis and that distinguish your passage from all others. Their uniqueness does not, however, define the form. The form is defined rather by
what is typical or shared with other passages.

5.4. Suggest a life setting.

Try to link the passage (in the sense of its form or forms) with the
real situation of its use. Sometimes the text itself does this for you.
Otherwise, you must work inferentially and with caution. It may be
obvious that a prophet has borrowed the funeral dirge form from the
life situation of funerals, and reused the form in a prophetic way, e.g.,
singing a predictive funeral dirge for Israel, which is to be destroyed
by Yahweh. But it is not so obvious where the life setting of a "community lament" psalm is to be located. Knowing the original life setting (often called the *Sitz im Leben*) usually helps you to understand
the passage in a concrete way. But an overemphasis on the life setting
can be counterproductive. The fact that a psalm, for example, has the
form of a royal accession song should not lead to the conclusion that
it has no function or meaning in the OT (or among Christians today)
other than as a part of the ancient Jerusalem coronation ritual. Its
original setting as a form is one thing; its potential for adaptation and
reuse for a whole variety of secondary settings (literary, cultural,
theological, etc.) is another. Try, then, to balance a sensitivity to the
theoretical origin of the form with its actual use in the context of your
passage.

5.5. Analyze the completeness of the form.

Compare your passage to other passages that have the same form.
In the particular instance of your passage, how completely is the
given form represented? Are all its usual elements present? If so, is
there also anything extraneous to the form that is present? If not,
what elements are lacking? Are they lacking because the passage is
logically elliptical (it leaves certain obvious elements unexpressed) or
because it is purposely modified? Does the ellipsis or modification
tell you anything about what the passage is focusing on or what its
special emphases are? The differences between your passage and all
others of the same essential form are what make your passage unique
and give it its special function in the Bible. Try to understand as well
as you can that uniqueness and that function.

Does your passage contain more than one form, as many passages do? If so, how are the forms to be separated out? Does the passage contain a mixture of forms or a form within a form (e.g., a riddle within a dream account, or a messenger speech within a woe oracle)? Or is your passage part of a larger form, the full extent of which goes beyond the limits of your passage? If so, what part does your passage and its form(s) play in the greater form?

5.6. Be alert to partial and broken forms.

Most of the time, all the known elements of a given form will not be present in any specific instance of its use. The more common the form, the more likely it may be that the form is partial, i.e., containing only some of all the possible elements that might be found in the fullest, most complete exemplar of such a form. For example, when the prophets repeat the word of Yahweh in the *rîb* (lawsuit) form, they often present only one aspect, such as the speech of indictment or the judgment sentence. Presumably their audiences recognized immediately from the partial form that a divine lawsuit was being described, in the same way that we can recognize from just the words "We interrupt this broadcast to bring you . . ." the form used today when an important news story is breaking. A partial form functions to suggest the purpose, tone, style, and audience of the full form without the needless detail and bulk necessitated by the full form. A form may also be broken (segmented) by the inclusion of other material within the form so that its constituent parts are rather widely separated from one another. Sometimes the beginning and end of a form are used to sandwich in material technically extraneous to the form proper. Such a sandwiching is known as an *inclusio*. The material sandwiched in such an *inclusio* is usually related to but not technically part of the form. Try to analyze the effect of any such structure on the interpretation of the passage.

Be careful about historical assessment and atomization. Considerable criticism has been leveled against these two past practices of many form critics. Historical assessment was the practice of calling into question some or all of the accuracy of the historical content in a given form, on the theory that certain kinds of forms preserved more genuine historical data than others. Atomization was the practice of assuming that the most basic forms were found in the smallest units—e.g., those of a verse or two in length—and that larger units were secondary. Both of these practices rested on assumptions that are now widely considered questionable. You should avoid them in your own exegesis.

6. Structure

6.1. Outline the passage.

Try to construct an outline that genuinely represents the major units of information. In other words, the outline should be a natural, not artificial, outgrowth of the passage. Note how many components are included under each topic (quantitative) and also the intensity or overall significance of the components (qualitative). Let the passage speak for itself. When you see a new topic, subject, issue, concept, or the like, you should construct a new topic for your outline. There are no automatic criteria for outlining. Don't be fooled by suggestions that you can count repetitions or identify "transitional" words (such as לָכֵן, "therefore") and mechanically derive your passage's outline. Your outline must instead be your best judgment as to how the major units of information in the passage group together logically. Some learning theorists suggest that the best outlines will contain from three to five major units, since most people have difficulty comprehending or remembering six or more abstract elements at once, and fewer than three elements hardly constitute an adequately descriptive outline. However, your outline must be a reflection of your best judgment about the logical structure of your passage, and the number of elements in the outline must reflect therefore the major units of information, however many they may be.

After outlining the major divisions, work on the more minor divisions, such as sentences, clauses, and phrases. These should, of course, be visibly subordinated under the major divisions. The outline should be as detailed as you can make it without seeming forced or artificial. From the outline you can then go on to make observations about the overall structure.

6.2. Look for patterns.

Any biblical passage whose limits have been properly identified will have a self-consistent logic made up of meaningful thought patterns. Try to identify the patterns, looking especially for such key features as developments, resumptions, unique forms of phrase, central or pivotal words, parallelisms, chiasms, *inclusios*, and other repetitious or progressive patterns. The keys to patterns are most often *repetition* and *progression*. Look for any evidence of repetition of a concept, word, phrase, expression, root, sound, or other identifiable feature and analyze the order of the repetition. Do the same with progressions, analyzing them as well. From this analysis may come very helpful insights. Poetry, by its very nature, will often contain more (and more striking) structural patterns than will prose. But any passage, properly defined, has structural patterns that should be analyzed and the results interpreted for your reader. Especially point out the unexpected or unique, since these are part of what makes your passage different from any other, and thus contribute to its special character and meaning.

6.3. Organize your discussion of structure according to descending units of size.

First discuss the overall outline pattern, i.e., the three to five (or more) major units. Then discuss that which you feel is important among the subpatterns within the major units, one at a time. Move from largest to smallest, i.e., from passage to paragraphs, to verses, to clauses, to words, to sounds in order. Where possible, describe whether you feel that a pattern is primary, secondary, or simply minor, and how important it is to the interpretation of the passage.

6.4. Evaluate the intentionality of the minor patterns.

Given enough time, most people can find all sorts of not very obvious minor patterns in a passage: a preponderance of certain vowel sounds here, the repetition of a verbal root there, the occurrence of a certain word exactly so many words after another word in two different verses, etc. The question is: Did these minor patterns happen to appear at random (according to what some people call the "law of averages"), or were they constructed intentionally by the ancient inspired speaker or writer? We assume that the major patterns, because they are so obvious, were intentional. We also assume that many minor patterns were intentional, especially when we can see such patterns occurring repeatedly throughout a given OT book or portion thereof or in parallels from other books. But how to be sure? There is only one criterion: Ask whether it is likely that the ancient speaker/writer composed the pattern for a purpose, and/or whether the ancient reader/hearer could reasonably be expected to have noticed the pattern as he/she listened to or read the passage. If it is likely in your judgment that the answer is yes, then evaluate the pattern as an intentional one. If no, then identify the pattern as probably unintentional or the like, and be cautious about making exegetical inferences from it.

6.5. If the passage is poetic, analyze accordingly.

Using semantic (meaning) parallelism as the guide, arrange the lines of poetry in parallel one to another. Then attempt to identify the meter of each line. If you can, revocalize the text to reflect the original pronunciation as much as possible, and describe the meter according to syllables per line (the most accurate method). Otherwise, describe the meter according to accents (less precise but still helpful). Note any special metrical features or patterns. Note any groupings suggested by the metrical count. Although the concepts of stanza and strophe are not native to Hebrew poetry, you may divide a poem into sections or parts if such a division actually seems to you inherent in the poem, based on a shift of scene, topic, or style. Rhyme or acrostic patterns are rare but deserve careful attention if present. Watch also for formulas (words or phrases used in more than one place in the OT, in like metrical contexts and patterns, to express a given idea). Formulas are "stock phrases" of poetry, especially musical poetry. Compare the use of a given formula in your passage with its use elsewhere. (See also step 8.) Watch also for epiphora (repetition of final sounds or words) and other patterns that frequently appear in poetry. Identify any intentional instances of assonance (repetition or juxtaposition of similar sounds), paronomasia (word play, including puns), *figura etymologica* (variation on word roots, often including names), and other such poetic devices. However, don't look for rhyme. Because so many Hebrew words have similar endings (most feminine singulars ending in –ah, most feminine plurals ending in –oth, most masculine plurals ending in –im), rhyme was too easy and would have been considered "cheap." Other poetic devices were far better tests of a poet's skill and indicated to an audience quality in poetic expression in a way that rhyme simply could not.

7. Grammatical Data

7.1. Analyze the significant grammatical issues.

A correct understanding of the grammar is essential to a proper interpretation of the passage. Are any grammatical points in doubt? Could any sentences, clauses, or phrases be read differently if the grammar were construed differently? Are you sure you have given proper weight to the nuances of meaning inherent in the specific verb conjugations and not merely the verbal roots? Slight variations in syntax can convey significant variations in meaning. Are the syntactical formations in your passage clearly understood? Does your translation need revision or annotation accordingly? Are there genuine ambiguities that make a definite interpretation of some part of the passage impossible? If so, what at least are the possible options? Is the grammar anomalous (not what would be expected) at any point? If so, can you offer any explanation for the anomaly? Pay attention also to ellipsis, asyndeton, prostaxis, parataxis, anacoluthon, and other special grammatical features that relate to interpretation. (See Soulen's *Handbook*—mentioned in the Introduction—for definitions.)

7.2. Analyze the orthography and morphology for date or other affinities.

All major texts of the Hebrew Bible contain an orthography (spelling style) characteristic of the Persian period (postexilic), since the texts selected for official status by the rabbis of the first century A.D. were apparently copies from the Persian period. At many important points, however, traces of older orthographies are discernible (see Cross and Freedman, *Early Hebrew Orthography* [4.7.2]). Does the passage have any of these, or traces of special ancient morphological features? Morphology refers to meaning-affecting parts of words, such as suffixes and prefixes. (For examples, see David A. Robertson, *Linguistic Evidence in Dating Early Hebrew Poetry*; Scholars Press, 1973.) If so, they may help indicate the date or even geographical origin of your passage, and may by their presence elsewhere help you to classify your passage in comparison to others. *Note*: At least an intermediate-level knowledge of Hebrew is required for this task.

8. Lexical Data

8.1. Explain all words and concepts that are not obvious.

Bear in mind that there is a difference between a word and a concept. A given concept may be expressed by many different words or wordings. An excellent reminder of this is Jesus' parable of the Good Samaritan in Luke 10. He tells the parable in order to demonstrate what it means to love neighbor as self, yet the parable does not contain the word "love" or "neighbor" or "self"—even though it contains powerfully the *concept* of loving neighbor as self. It is important therefore to realize that your purpose in analyzing the lexical data is to understand the individual concepts of your passage, whether these concepts are conveyed by single words, groups of words, or by the way that all the words are put together into a coherent pericope.

Work in descending order of size from whole sentences or even groups of sentences (if applicable) through clauses (if applicable) through phrases (such as idioms) to words and parts of words. Using the various helps available (see 4.8), try to define for your reader any concepts, words, or wordings that might not be clear or whose force would not be noticed without attention being called to them. Some of these explanations may be very brief, others fairly detailed. Proper nouns almost always deserve some attention. So do idioms, since by definition an idiom is a wording that *cannot* be translated literally, i.e., word for word. When citing words from the passage, use either the Hebrew letters or an underlined transliteration of them.

8.2. Concentrate on the most important concepts, words, and wordings.

Working in descending order of size, isolate whatever you consider especially significant or pivotal for the interpretation of the passage. Assemble a list of perhaps six to twelve such important concepts, words, or wordings. Try to rank them in order from most crucial to least crucial. Focus on these, telling your reader why they are important to the interpretation. The meaning of a passage is built up from the meaning of its concepts, and the more clearly they are explained, the more clearly the passage is likely to be understood.

8.3. Do "word studies" (really, concept studies) of the most crucial words or wordings.

Using the procedure outlined in 4.8.3, try to analyze the most crucial—therefore not a large number—of the key words or wordings in the passage. Present a summary of your procedures and findings to the reader. (Much of the statistical or procedural information may be relegated to footnotes.) Do not neglect the specific theological meaning(s) of words or wordings in considering the various ranges of meaning. In addition, be sure that you don't merely analyze individual words, but also words in combination—including combinations that are sometimes separated from one another by intervening words—because combinations of words convey concepts as well. Be as inductive as possible, checking your conclusions against, rather than deriving them from, the theological dictionaries.

8.4. Identify any special semantic features.

The semantics (the relation between content and meaning) of the passage is often affected by such features as irony, anaphora, epiphora, paronomasia, metonymy, hendiadys, formulas, loanwords, purposeful archaizing, and etymological oddities. Look for these, and bring them to the attention of your reader. Where possible, show how they affect interpretation.

9. Biblical Context

At this point you must begin tentatively drawing together in your mind the essential discoveries from the previous sections for the purpose of focusing on the specific "message" of the passage as it relates more broadly to the message of both its immediate and its wider context. In other words, you can no longer pay attention only to individual features of the passage. How the passage as a complete entity actually fits into a broader body of truth now calls for attention.

You may find it helpful at this stage to summarize for yourself what you consider to be the passage's message—including its central point(s), essential characteristics, unmistakable implications, or the like. Such a summary is necessarily quite tentative, but it helps to focus your attention on the biblical and theological significance of the passage. The three procedures outlined next are designed to help you make headway as regards the passage's connections with the rest of Scripture, and the three that follow in step 10 should help you relate the passage to the more general discipline of dogmatic theology.

9.1. Analyze the use of the passage elsewhere in Scripture.

Is the passage or any part of it quoted or alluded to anywhere else in the Bible? How? Why? If more than once, how and why, and what are the differences, if any? What does the reference made elsewhere to the passage tell you about how it was interpreted? If it is alluded to, how does the allusion shed light on how the passage was understood within the context where the allusion is found? If it is quoted, how does the circumstance under which it is quoted aid in its interpretation? The mere fact that a portion of a passage is quoted elsewhere in Scripture may say much about its intended impact, its uniqueness, its foundational nature theologically, or the like.

9.2. Analyze the passage's relation to the rest of Scripture.

How does the passage function dogmatically (i.e., as teaching or conveying a message) in the section, book, division, Testament, Bible—in that order? Does it have any special relationships to any apocryphal or pseudepigraphic writings? How does it or its elements compare to other Scriptures that address the same sorts of issues? What is it similar or dissimilar to? It may be necessary to address these questions with various portions of the passage if in your judgment the various portions make individual assertions. But the primary goal is to see the message of the passage as a whole as it fits within the overall biblical revelation.

9.3. Analyze the passage's import for understanding Scripture.

What hinges on it elsewhere? What other elements in Scripture help make it comprehensible? Why? How? Does the passage affect the meaning or value of other Scriptures in a way that crosses literary or historical lines? Does the passage concern issues that are dealt with in the same or different ways elsewhere in Scripture? Does the passage exist primarily to reinforce what is already knowable from other portions of Scripture, or does it make a genuinely special contribution? Suppose the passage were not in the Bible at all. What would be lost or how would the message of the Bible be less complete if the passage did not exist?

10. Theology

10.1. Locate the passage theologically.

Where does the passage fit within the whole corpus of revelation comprising Christian (dogmatic) theology? Under which covenant does it fit? Are aspects of it limited in part or in whole to the Old Covenant as, for example, certain cultic sacrificial practices or certain rules for tribal responsibilities would be? If so, is it still relevant as a historical example of God's relationship to human beings, or as an indication of God's holiness, standards, justice, immanence, transcendence, compassion, etc.? (The reason theology is called theology reflects the fact that the better one understands God, the better one understands what life is about, what truths and practices are essential or important, and what values best protect against disobedience to God. One can understand much about God from the covenant God revealed to Israel even if various aspects of that covenant are superseded by the New Covenant.) Is the passage related to far broader theological concerns that encompass both covenants and are not strictly bound by either? To which doctrine(s) does the passage relate? Does it have potential relevance for the classical doctrinal conceptions of God, humanity, angels, sin, salvation, the church, eschatology, etc.? Does it relate to these areas of doctrine because of its vocabulary or subject matter, or perhaps because of something less explicit? (A passage that shows the nature of the love of God for us may not happen to mention love, God, or us directly.)

10.2. Identify the specific issues raised or solved by the passage.

Go beyond the general areas of doctrine that are touched on in the passage and identify the specific issues. What in fact are the prob-

lems, blessings, concerns, confidences, etc. about which the passage
has something to say? How does the passage speak to these? How
clearly are they dealt with in the passage? Is the passage one that
raises apparent difficulties for some doctrines while solving others?
If so, try to deal with this situation systematically and also in a manner that is helpful to your readers.

10.3. Analyze the theological contribution of the passage.

What does the passage contain that contributes to the solution of
doctrinal questions or supports solutions offered elsewhere in Scripture? How major or minor is the passage's contribution? How certain
can you be that the passage, properly understood, has the theological significance you propose to attach to it? Does your approach agree
with that of other scholars or theologians who are known to have
addressed themselves to the passage? How does the passage conform theologically to the entire system of truth contained in Christian theology? (It is a basic and, indeed, necessary assumption that a
proper theology should be consistent overall and univocal—i.e.,
coherent and non-contradictory.) How does your passage comport
with the greater theological whole? In what way might it be important precisely for that whole? Does it function to counterbalance or
correct any questionable or extreme theological position? Is there
anything about the passage that does not seem readily to relate to a
particular expression of Christian theology? (Remember that the
Scripture is primary and theological systems are secondary.) What
solution can you offer for any problems, even tentatively? If a solution is not readily forthcoming, why? Is it because the passage is
obscure, or because you lack knowledge, or because the presump-
tions and speculations required would perhaps be too great to be convincing? The Bible contains some things that from a human point of
view may seem difficult to comprehend, or even paradoxical. Does
your passage deal with an area where there are so many unknowns
that you must refrain from trying to identify some aspects of its theological contribution? If so, your reader deserves to be told this, but
in a constructive rather than a destructive way. Do everything you
can to milk the passage for its theological value, but do not force anything from or into the passage.

11. Secondary Literature

11.1. Investigate what others have said about the passage.

Even though you will have consulted commentaries, grammars, and many kinds of other books and articles in the process of completing the preceding ten steps, you should now undertake a more systematic investigation of the secondary literature that may apply to your passage. In order for the exegesis to be *your* work and not merely a mechanical compendium of others' views, it is wise to do your own thinking and to arrive at your own conclusions as much as possible prior to this step. Otherwise, you are not so much doing an exegesis of the passage as you are evaluating others' exegeses—and therefore helping to guarantee that you will not go beyond that which they have achieved.

Now, however, is the proper time to ask what various scholars think about the passage. What points have they made that you overlooked? What have they said better? What have they given more weight to? Or, conversely, what do you feel you must reject in their views? Can you point out things that they have said that are questionable or incorrect? If in your opinion any of these scholars is to be disagreed with, point this out using the footnotes for minor differences and the body of the paper for more significant ones. Note: As a rule, it is considered far more convincing to disagree with a scholar's views if you have also given him or her proper commendation for those views of his or hers on your passage that you do agree with, and to state your own conclusions modestly rather than stridently.

11.2. Compare and adjust.

Have the conclusions of other scholars helped you to change your analysis in any way? Do other scholars analyze the passage or any aspects of it in a manner that is more incisive or that leads to a more satisfying set of conclusions? Do they organize their exegesis in a better way? Do they give consideration to implications you hadn't even considered? Do they supplement your own findings? If so, do not hesitate to revise your own conclusions or procedures in steps 1 through 10, giving proper credit in each case. But never feel that you must cover in your exegesis everything that the others do. Reject what does not seem germane, and limit what seems out of proportion. You decide, not they.

11.3. Apply your discoveries throughout your paper.

Do not include a separate section of findings from secondary literature in any draft of your paper. Do not view this step as resulting in a single block of material within the paper. Step 11 is, in other words, a step in your research process but not in your final written product. Your discoveries should produce additions or corrections, or both, at many points throughout the exegesis. Try to be sure that a change or addition at one point does not contradict statements made elsewhere in the paper. Consider the implications of all changes. For example, if you adjust the textual analysis (step 1) on the basis of what you have now learned from something in the secondary literature, how will this affect the translation, lexical data, and other parts of the exegesis? Aim for consistency and evenness throughout. This will influence considerably the reader's ability to appreciate your conclusions. Carefully give due credit to secondary sources in the footnotes and bibliography.

12. Application

Everyone agrees that exegesis seeks to determine the meaning of a passage of Scripture. Many exegetes believe, however, that their responsibilities stop with the past—that exegesis is the attempt to discover what the text *meant*, not what it *means* now. Placing such arbitrary limits on exegesis is unsatisfactory for three reasons. First, it ignores the ultimate reason why the vast majority of people engage in exegesis or are interested in the results of exegesis: They desire to hear and obey God's word as it is found in the passage. Exegesis, in other words, is an empty intellectual entertainment when divorced from application. Second, it addresses only one aspect of meaning—the historical—as if God's words were intended only for individual generations and not also for us and, indeed, for those who will follow us in time. The Scriptures are *our* Scriptures, not just the Scriptures of the ancients. Finally, it leaves the actual personal or corporate existential interpretation and use of the passage to subjectivity. The exegete, who has come to know the passage best, refuses to help the reader or hearer of the passage at the very point where the reader's or hearer's interest is keenest. The exegete leaves the key function—response—completely to the subjective sensibilities of the reader or hearer, who knows the passage least. Naturally, the exegete cannot actually control what the reader does in response to the passage. But the exegete can—and must—do his or her best to define the areas within which a faithful response will be found and to suggest, if necessary, areas of response that the passage might seem on the surface to call for but that are not justified by the results of the exegesis.

Making decisions about application is more an art than a science; it is qualitative, not quantitative. Nevertheless, the following procedural steps will help you isolate the applicable issues of the passage systematically and will maximize your chances of relating those issues properly to the persons or groups for whom your exegesis should have benefit. An application should be just as rigorous, just as thorough, and just as analytically sound as any other step in the exegesis process. It cannot be merely tacked on to the rest of the exegesis as a sort of spiritual afterthought. Moreover, it must carefully reflect the data of the passage if it is to be convincing. Your reader needs to see how you derived the application as the natural and final stage of the entire process of careful, analytical study (exegesis) of your passage.

Subjectivity is the primary enemy of good application. When people think that they can derive from a passage an application that is somehow relevant to them but not to others, or is somehow unique to one passage but not even comparable to the applications of closely similar passages, the probability of logical consistency is reduced and the likelihood of accuracy is therefore threatened.

Objectivity in application is best assured by following the sort of systematic process outlined next. See also (on page 177) the list of the most common hermeneutical fallacies that undermine the likelihood of proper application.

12.1. List the life issues.

A starting point for the proper application of a passage is comparing life issues. To apply a passage you must try to decide what its central issues are and what issues in it are only secondary. In other words, what aspect(s) of life is the passage really concerned with?

You must try to decide how such issues are or are not still active in the lives of persons or groups today. What do "I" or "we" encounter today that is similar or at least related to what the passage deals with? The life issues will emerge from the exegetical data on the one hand, and from your own knowledge of the world on the other.

Identify first all potential life issues included in the passage. Then identify those issues transferable from the passage to the current situation, using the following steps to help make the transfer accurate. The audience for whom you are doing your exegesis can have an effect on the way you isolate the issues but should not per se change the issues themselves.

12.2. Clarify the nature of the application (does it inform or direct?).

Applications may generally be of two kinds: those which basically *inform* the reader and those which basically *direct* the reader. A passage that functions to describe some aspect of the love of God might be considered primarily to inform. A passage that functions to command the reader to love God wholeheartedly primarily directs. Obviously there is considerable overlap between informing and directing, and a passage can contain elements that are at the same time informative and directive. Nevertheless, the force of your application will be much clearer and more specific if you divide the applicability in this way, at least tentatively. At first, maximize—include all the possibilities, knowing that you will discard some or most later, after more analysis. Caution: Narrative passages do not generally teach something directly; rather, they illustrate what is taught directly elsewhere.

12.3. Clarify the possible areas of application (faith or action).

Applications may fall into two general areas: *faith* and *action*. In practice, faith and action should ultimately be inseparable—a genuine Christian could not display one without the other. But even though they must belong together in the Christian's life, faith and action may be considered distinct entities, and a given passage, part or whole, may concentrate on one more than the other. Try therefore to decide the potential areas of application for the material contained in the passage, dividing tentatively into categories of faith and action. Be inclusive at first; reject and discard later.

12.4. Identify the audience of the application.

There are primarily two audiences to whom the application(s) may be seen to be directed: the personal and the corporate. What in the passage gives information or direction regarding faith or action to individuals? What to groups or corporate structures? If such a differentiation cannot be made, why not?

If the passage informs or directs individuals, what kind of individuals are they? Christian or non-Christian? Laypersons or clergypersons? Parents or children? Powerful or weak? Haughty or humble? Desperate or confident? What in the passage makes this clear? How does the passage address the object of its informing or directing? If the passage informs or directs groups or corporate entities, which kind are they? Church? Nation? Clergy? A profession? A societal structure? A family? People who are closely allied? People who are at enmity with one another? Some other group or combination of groups?

12.5. Establish the categories of the application.

Is the application directed toward matters that are primarily personal in nature or primarily interpersonal in nature? Matters that relate to sin, or perhaps to doubt, or perhaps to proper piety? Or to the relationship of God and people? Is the concern social, economic, moral, religious, spiritual, familial, financial, etc.?

12.6. Determine the time focus of the application.

Does the passage call primarily for a recognition of something that occurred in the past? Does it expect present faith or action? Does it look primarily to the future? Does the application involve a combination of times? Is there a concern for immediate action? Or is what is called for more a matter of steady response over a long period of time? Does the timing of the application depend on the nature of the audience or some other factor?

12.7. Fix the limits of the application.

It is often as valuable to explain how a passage does not apply as to explain how it does. Does the passage call for a response that could possibly be misunderstood and then taken too far? If so, how can you define what is too far? Does the passage call for an application that is secondary rather than primary? That is, does your passage function more as a background or support, or part of a further or larger passage which more specifically suggests an application than does your passage? Is your passage one of several that all function together to suggest a given application which none of them individually would quite have, or at least quite have in the same way? Are there any applications which at first might seem appropriate to the passage but which upon more careful examination are not? If so, briefly identify these for your reader and give your reasoning. Does the passage have a double application, as for example certain messianic passages do—one application having immediate reference, the other having more of a long-range reference? If so, are both applications of equal weight now? Were they of equal weight when the passage was first spoken or written?

In general, it is probably safest to limit potential applications as much as possible. Rare is the passage that calls for several applications, all of equal relevance or practicability. Try to decide what one application is most central to and follows most naturally from the passage. If you are convinced that the passage demands more than one application, at least try to rank these in order of either universality of application or urgency of application. Remember: You are not responsible for discussing all the possible ways in which the passage might strike the fancy of the reader or be put to use—wisely or not—by the reader. Rather, you are responsible for educating the reader about what the passage *itself* calls for or leads to in terms of application. If the passage is so brief or specialized that you are at a loss to suggest any application for it (even as part of a greater whole), you would be wiser to suggest no application than to suggest one that is ultimately unsound. By all means, an application must derive demonstrably from the data of the passage and not from preconceived notions to which the passage is then forced to conform.

Moving from Outline to Paper

After completing the research in step-by-step fashion, you will want to organize the results into a format that presents them effectively to the reader.

There are many acceptable formats. If a given one is specified for you by a professor or editor, you will obviously follow that. Otherwise you might wish to consider using one of the three most common options. The first is the topical format, which proceeds much in the same order as the twelve steps above, but with sections and headings rearranged, combined, expanded, or otherwise adjusted according to your own best sense of how the material of the passage can be drawn convincingly to the attention of the reader. The second is the commentary format, which moves more or less verse by verse through the passage, marshaling relevant data and conclusions as they apply to individual parts of the passage, yet not excluding appropriate additional sections, such as introductions, excursuses, and summaries. The third is the unitary format, in which the passage is discussed in a relatively free-flowing fashion, apart from a strictly systematic or methodical outline, with or without the use of formally identified sections, subsections, headings, and so forth.

Any of these formats—and many others—can serve you well. Do not hesitate to be innovative, as long as the format you choose aids in getting the full impact of your findings across to your readers.

II

Exegesis
and the Original Text

THE PURPOSE OF THIS CHAPTER is to help you get a better feel for the process of exegesis by providing illustrations of how certain parts of the process might work in various OT passages. A good many passages are used selectively here—in some instances more than one for a given exegesis step—in an effort to provide you with an exposure to the OT's rich diversity of material. Therefore you will not see a systematic exegetical coverage of any single passage; for examples of the latter, recent technical, exegetical commentaries such as the Word Biblical Commentary series or the Hermeneia series (see 4.11.4) will prove helpful, as will, occasionally, the exegesis articles in a journal such as *Interpretation* (4.11.2).

Those who cannot read Hebrew will still find the content of this chapter helpful and generally comprehensible. For those who know Hebrew, regular reference to *BHS* is essential for a sense of the full contexts from which this chapter's selections are taken.

For convenience, the divisions in this chapter correspond to those in chapter 1. Not every step should require an illustration, but wherever one might genuinely be helpful, at least one has been provided. Longer or multiple illustrations have been provided when it seemed that they might help clarify the exegesis process.

1. Text

1.1. Confirming the limits of the passage

There are two places to which you can turn immediately for help in confirming proper limits for a passage: (1) the Hebrew text itself in *BHS* (or *BH3*), and (2) virtually any modern translation. It is their paragraphing that you want to examine. In the case of the Hebrew text, the biblical material is set off in paragraph form by means of right-margin indentation variation. When the margin location changes, either by going further into the middle of the page or by going further back out to the right edge, that is signaling the editor's opinion that a new logical section has begun. In the case of the modern English versions, simple indentation of the first word in a sentence indicates a new paragraph. By examining the arrangement of your passage, ideally both in Hebrew and English, you can tell quickly whether your own tentative identification of a passage conforms to scholars' judgments about the natural groupings of subject matter.

Decisions about paragraphing are sometimes subjective, and you will find that the various editors' groupings of content do not always agree. But if you decide to start your passage where no editor has begun a paragraph, or end your passage where no editor has ended a paragraph, then it is your responsibility to argue fully for your decision to select or configure the passage as you have done.

1.2. Comparing the versions

To analyze the various versions of the OT, you must in effect translate each one back into Hebrew at least to the extent that you can tell whether it reflects the MT or runs contrary to it. Since this process can be complicated, most people find it helpful, at least at first, to chart the versions one above another, line by line, so that your ability to compare readings is facilitated. Remember to compare the wording of the versions for the whole passage. If you try to consult the versions only when the MT seems problematic, you will miss all the variants that resulted from MT corruptions that once were obvious but later were smoothed over and rewritten into readable Hebrew (but not necessarily the original Hebrew) by well-meaning scribes of old.

A word-by-word comparison in the case of 1 Samuel 20:32 (where the Qumran version happens to exist) would look something like the chart on the next page.

By writing out the Hebrew of the MT, then listing selected versions (including the LXX) directly underneath, according to the Semitic word order from right to left, you can easily see how the versions line up. In the chart, the parentheses are a convenient way to indicate that both the Qumran text and the LXX omit any correspondence to the MT אליו, suggesting that this word might be an expansion (in this case, a simple explanatory addition) in the MT. However, the LXX also omits any correspondence to the MT and Qumran words אביו ויאמר. This perhaps reflects a haplography (a loss of something once present) in the Hebrew text that was used by the LXX translator. The Peshitta and Targum follow the MT, as they usually do. The Vulgate, typically, follows the MT. (The Peshitta, Targum, and Vulgate are much less often true "independent" witnesses to an original that differs from the MT than the LXX is. Even the Qumran scrolls, themselves Hebrew, will much more often reflect independence from the Hebrew MT than the Peshitta, Targum, or Vulgate will.)

In the chart, we have included the English translation according to the Semitic word order. You may find it helpful to do this, at least as you begin learning the method. You may also wish to include the English translation under any spot where the versions contain a different wording from the MT, especially if you cannot translate the various versions at sight! Refer to Brotzman's *Old Testament Textual Criticism: A Practical Introduction* or Tov's *Textual Criticism of the Hebrew Bible* or McCarter's *Textual Criticism: Recovering the Text of the Hebrew Bible* (see 4.1.2) for examples and explanations of the principles involved in deciding which version best reflects the original.

1.3. Reconstructing and annotating the text

Two examples are given here to illustrate the process of reconstructing and annotating the text. Many times a passage will require no reconstruction at all. After you have compared the versions, you will decide that the passage as printed in the *BHS* or *BH3* (both contain the wording of the Leningrad Codex of A.D. 1008) adequately preserves the original. But when the ancient versions disagree

I Samuel 20:32

	And answered	Jonathan	Saul	his father
MT	ויען	יהונתן	את שאול	אביו
Qumran	[first two words obliterated]		"	( )
LXX	καὶ ἀπεκρίθη	Ιωναθαν	τῷ Σαουλ	"
(MT) Syriac	"	"	"	"
(MT) Targum	"	"	"	"
(MT) Vulgate	"	"	"	"

	and said	to him	Why	must he die?	What	has he done?
MT	ויאמר	אליו	למה	יומת	מה	עשה
Qumran	"	( )	"	"	"	"
LXX	( )	( )	ἵνα τί	ἀποθνῄσκει;	τί	πεποίηκεν;
(MT) Syriac	"	"	"	"	"	"
(MT) Targum	"	"	"	"	"	"
(MT) Vulgate	"	"	"	"	"	"

significantly, you must attempt to determine how that disagreement might have arisen. That is, you must look for an original wording that would best account for the present divergent wordings. This means working backward from what is present in the various ancient versions to what theoretically must have been in the original text.

Hundreds of differences in translation among modern English versions of the OT are due simply to translators' reconstructions of the Hebrew text. No modern translation follows the *BHS/BH3* Hebrew text slavishly. All translators change it whenever they think that the evidence from the ancient versions points to an original Hebrew text different from that preserved in the Leningrad Codex. As a result, they are often translating into English from a *reconstructed* Hebrew text. Thus, if for no other reason than to understand why modern translators have done what they have done, you need to know something about how reconstructing a text works. The examples below should help.

Reconstructing two Hebrew names: Joshua 7:1

A careful comparison of the ancient versions confirms what the *BHS* textual footnotes 1a and 1b alert you to in abbreviated form. That is, the Hebrew (MT)

עָכָן בֶּן־כַּרְמִי בֶן־זַבְדִּי

is possibly the result of a miscopy at some point in the long history of the transmission of the text of Joshua. For the name עָכָן (Achan) you find that a number of important Septuagint (Greek) texts, as well as the Syriac Peshitta, have the equivalent of עָכָר (Achar), which is the form this name has in the Hebrew text as well, at 1 Chronicles 2:7. Moreover, the name of this person's grandfather, זַבְדִּי (Zabdi) in the Hebrew, is rendered in a number of important Septuagint texts as the equivalent of זִמְרִי (Zimri), which is also the form the name has in 1 Chronicles 2:6.

Which is correct: Achan grandson of Zabdi or Achar grandson of Zimri? Three considerations help you decide. First, you take the approach that the Greek (LXX) evidence must be evaluated seriously. (See 4.1.3 for further comment on the value of the LXX relative to the MT.) It makes the choice at least a toss-up. The addition of Syriac evidence in the instance of the first name adds even more weight.

Second, you note that the comparative readings in Chronicles are very strong evidence for Achar and Zimri, respectively. Why? Because the Chronicler, writing long after the book of Joshua was complete, reflects an independent rendering of the names. We have no evidence to suggest that the Chronicler would alter a name, and plenty to suggest that his concern for accurate genealogies might preserve a name more precisely than even the book of Joshua would. Third, you see that the passage makes an issue of the mnemonic device, a pun, by which Israelites remembered the valley where Achan/Achar was stoned. They called it (Josh. 7:26) עֵמֶק עָכוֹר, "Trouble Valley," the word for "trouble" (עָכוֹר, Achor) having the same consonants as Achar, but not those of Achan.

You must then give this evidence and your reasoning (whether briefly or at length depends on the scope of your paper) for the originality of Achar and Zimri, in annotations to the text you print in your paper. Using the bracket system recommended in chapter 1, you may make your reconstructed text look something like this:

$$\text{וַיִּקַּח עָכָ}{>}\text{ר}{<}^{a}\text{ בֶּן־כַּרְמִי בֶּן־ זִ }{>}\text{ מְר }{<}^{b}$$

The superscript letters [a] and [b] will alert the reader to look for explanations of these reconstructions in your annotations.

Reconstructing a common term: 1 Samuel 8:16

Near the middle of the verse, the Hebrew (MT) reads:

וְאֶת־בַּחוּרֵיכֶם הַטּוֹבִים

and your fine/choice young men

A careful examination of the ancient versions reveals to you, however, that the Greek (LXX) at the same point in the verse has

τὰ βουκόλια ὑμῶν τὰ ἀγαθὰ

your fine/choice cattle

Which was the original—"cattle" or "young men" or neither—and how do you decide? First, following the most basic principle of text

criticism (as explained for you in any of the basic guides to text criticism listed in 4.1.2), you try to determine what original wording
would, in the history of copying/miscopying the passage, have produced both "young men" in the Hebrew and "cattle" in the Greek. To
do this you must translate the Greek back into Hebrew, because the
original wording was not Greek but Hebrew. Here, by consulting
Hatch and Redpath's *A Concordance to the Septuagint* (see 4.8.2) or by
using one of the sophisticated computer concordances to trace
Hebrew equivalents for Greek words (see 4.8.2) you can find at once
that βουκόλια is how the LXX frequently translated the Hebrew בָּקָר,
cattle."

Now, just two more steps. First, you compare בָּחוּר and בָּקָר. The
words are the same except for the middle consonant, ח or ק. The *shureq*
vowel (וּ), though written with *waw*, is only a vowel and represents a
vocalization decision by copyists long after 1 Samuel was first written (cf. Cross and Freedman, *Early Hebrew Orthography* [4.7.2]). What
original word would account for both בָּחוּר and בָּקָר? Your answer is:
בָּקָר, "cattle." The ח of בחור is probably the miscopy. Second, you confirm this decision by analyzing the immediate context. After "male
slaves" and "female slaves" (a logical pair), "young men" and "donkeys" would hardly go together. But "cattle" and "donkeys," another
logical pair, certainly would.

Finally, you summarize the evidence and your reasoning for your
reader, at whatever length is appropriate to your paper. Your reconstructed text might look like this:

וְאֶת־בְּ קָק<a> רֵיכרם הַטּוֹבִים

The [a] would refer the reader to your annotation, i.e., your summary of the textual evidence and explanation, in the footnotes or
endnotes.

1.4. Putting your passage in versified form

To save space, the *BHS* (as did *BH3*) arranges poetry so that an
entire couplet (bicolon) or triplet (tricolon) appears on one printed
line. But in an exegesis paper it is usually better to list each part of a
couplet or triplet on a line of its own. This way the correspondences
from line to line are much more evident.

Here is Numbers 23:8–9 versified in such a manner:

How can I curse
    whom God has not cursed?
And how can I denounce
    whom Yahweh has not denounced?

⁸מָה אֶקֹּב לֹא קַבֹּה אֵל

וּמָה אֶזְעֹם לֹא זָעַם יהוה

For from the tops of the mountains
    I see him,
And from the hills I view him.

⁹כִּי־מֵרֹאשׁ צֻרִים אֶרְאֶבּוּ

וּמִגְּבָעוֹת אֲשׁוּרֶנּוּ

Look, the people dwells alone
And among the nations
    does not consider itself.

הֶן־עָם לְבָדָד יִשְׁכֹּן

וּבַגּוֹיִם לֹא יִתְחַשָּׁב

From such an arrangement it is much easier to see that the couplet in v. 8 is a simple word-for-word synonymous parallelism, while the couplets in v. 9 represent more complicated synonymous parallelisms.

By the way, unless you actually intend to analyze the Masoretes' medieval chanting system or count their (chanting) accents as a rough way of analyzing the meter of a poem (see the Masora introductions by Kelley, et al. or Ginsburg in 4.1.2 for help in doing this if it is what you wish to do), there is no point in including the accent marks in your own written text.

2. Translation

The purpose of the following illustrations is to encourage you to produce your own translation of a passage rather than simply relying on translations found in major modern versions. These brief examples all involve relatively simple Hebrew wordings, which nevertheless have not always been translated clearly or even properly.

What right have you to disagree with translations produced by "experts"? You have every right! Consider the facts: All the modern translations (and all the ancient ones for that matter) have been produced either by committees working against time deadlines or by individuals who can't possibly know the whole Bible so well in the original that they produce flawless renderings at every point. More-

over, in the modern business of Bible publishing, the more "different" a translation is, the more risk there is that it won't sell. Thus there
is a pressure on translators, committees, publishers, etc., to keep renderings conservative in meaning, even though, happily, usually up-
to-date in idiomatic language. Finally, most people hate to go out on
a limb with a translation in print. Many translation problems are matters of ambiguity: There is more than one way to construe the original. But space limitations do not permit translators to offer an
explanation every time they might wish to render something from
the original in a truly new way. So they almost always err on the side
of caution. As a result, all modern translations tend, albeit with perfectly good intentions, to be overly "safe" and traditional. In the
working of a translation committee, the lone genius is usually out-
voted by the cautious majority.

Therefore, every so often you might actually produce a better
translation than others have done, because you can invest much more
time exegeting your passage than the individuals or committees were
able to because of the speed at which they were required to work.
Besides, you are choosing a translation suitable for your particular
reader(s) rather than for the whole English-speaking world. Remember: A word doesn't so much have an individual meaning as a *range
of meanings*. Choosing from that range of meanings is often subjective
and should be something *you* do for the benefit of your audience,
rather than something you leave entirely to others who have no
knowledge of your audience and must translate strictly for the
masses. Fortunately, in an exegesis paper you can explain briefly to
your reader, in the annotations to your translation, the options you
had to choose from, and your reason(s) for choosing the particular
English word that you did. Those who worked on the various ancient
or modern versions did not have such an opportunity.

2.1. A translation that clarifies a prophet's behavior: Jonah 1:2

וּקְרָא עָלֶיהָ כִּי־עָלְתָה רָעָתָם לְפָנָי

The usual translation of the last part of the verse is something like:
"proclaim against it because its evil has come up before me." This
translation, however, has always been problematic. It represents only
one way of rendering some Hebrew words that have extensive

ranges of meaning, and it doesn't fit easily the point of the overall
story. After all, this is a command that Jonah tries to disobey by refus-
ing to go to Nineveh. Yet as typically translated it sounds like a command Jonah would love to obey. Why wouldn't he be glad to preach
against a city God has declared to be *evil?*

In 1.2.1 you are advised to "start fresh, from the beginning." Following that advice, and determined not to accept the usual translation as the only reasonable option just because it is the usual one, you
consider the meaning of the Hebrew words afresh by looking at their
definitions in a good up-to-date lexicon such as Holladay or Koehler-
Baumgartner (4.8.1). Here is what you find: עַל can mean "against"
but also "concerning." כִּי can mean "because" but also "that." רָעָה can
mean "evil" but more commonly means "trouble." And עָלְה ... לְפָנַי is
best translated idiomatically not "come ... before me" but "come to
my attention." Eventually you conclude that the whole clause can
very well mean "proclaim concerning it that their trouble has come
to my attention."

The exegetical implications are significant. In contrast to the usual
translation, your translation makes it clear why the hypernationalist
Jonah fled from his assignment: God was sending him on a mission
of concern, not a mission of denunciation. A careful reading of the rest
of the book confirms this repeatedly (cf. especially Jonah 4).

2.2. A modest, noninterpretive translation: Proverbs 22:6

חֲנֹךְ לַנַּעַר עַל־פִּי דַרְכּוֹ
גַּם כִּי־יַזְקִין לֹא־יָסוּר מִמֶּנָּה

This verse is usually translated about as follows: "Train a child in
the way he should go, and when he is old he will not depart from it."
But when you analyze the words' meaning ranges closely, you find
no Hebrew equivalent for the English "should." This piques your
interest. After all, the usual translation seems to promise quite a lot.
Indeed, this rather popular verse has often been cited in support of
the notion that parents can virtually guarantee that their children will
turn out to be godly adults if raised properly. Most proverbs are of
course generalizations, and generalizations have their exceptions.
But you still have every right to "start fresh" in your own translation
of this proverb, no matter how well known it may be. (Remember:

The more well known a wording in the Bible is, the more hesitant modern professional translations are to depart from it, even when they dislike it, for fear that people will not buy a Bible that has changed the wording of one of their "favorite verses.")

The process of translating afresh is not a terribly complicated one. It requires mainly a willingness to consider combinations of meanings slowly and carefully. Thus with regard to Proverbs 22:6, what you can easily determine by patiently consulting a lexicon is that עַל־פִּי means "according to" and that דֶּרֶךְ means simply "way," so that דַּרְכּוֹ means either "his way" or "his own way." The first half of this poetic couplet actually says, then, "Train a child according to his (own) way." You still find nothing about "should" here. The real point of the verse, you conclude rightly, is that a child who is allowed selfishly to do what he or she wants when young will have the same selfish tendencies as an adult.

Note: Excellent sources of alternative translations are the authors' translations in technical commentaries. A scholar who has studied a book intensively is usually best equipped to offer a nuanced translation. And for late-breaking information on more precise meanings of individual Hebrew words, check the annual listing of words discussed in the articles abstracted in *Old Testament Abstracts* (4.11.1), either via its book or its computerized format.

3. Historical Context

The historical situation out of which or to which a portion of Scripture was written must be understood for that portion of Scripture to be fully meaningful. Of course, some passages are less strictly "historical" than others. The Twenty-third Psalm, for example, addresses concerns that almost anyone, at any time or place, has been able to appreciate. And Psalm 117, with its simple injunction to praise God and its declaration of God's loyalty ("Praise the LORD, all nations . . . ; the faithfulness of the Lord endures forever") is about as panhistorical and pancultural as biblical literature could be.

But knowing the background, social setting, foreground, geographical setting, and date are normally essential to appreciating the significance of a passage. Most OT passages contain material that relates strongly to such considerations. The Bible is such a historically oriented revelation that ignoring historical context tends to assure misinterpretation. A basic principle of hermeneutics (the science of interpretation) is that a passage cannot mean what it could never have meant. In other words, you must know which events, situations, times, persons, and places your passage is referring to if you are not to remove your passage from the very context that gives it its true meaning. The illustration below is chosen as an example of a passage whose meaning cannot be adequately appreciated unless proper attention is paid to its historical background, social setting, foreground, geographical setting, and date.

3.1. Context clarifies a prophecy: Hosea 5:8–10

At first glance this brief prophetic oracle is puzzling. Why such emphasis on horns (שׁוֹפָר, חֲצֹצְרָה) and alarm (הָרִיעוּ)? Why the deep concern about a boundary marker (גְּבוּל)? And why does all this make Yahweh proclaim his wrath (עֶבְרָתִי)?

When you follow the suggestions in 1.3, "Historical Context," here is what you find. First, consulting the Scripture reference index in virtually any of the major histories of Israel (see 4.3.2), you find that Hosea 5:8–10 has a clear historical referent: the counterattack by Judah against (northern) Israel in the Syro-Ephraimite War of 734–733 B.C. As you read beyond these sources in historically oriented commentaries and follow the geographical details via a good Bible atlas (4.3.6), you note the following (here only summarized):

Background. King Rezin of Aram-Damascus and King Pekah of Israel had approached King Ahaz of Judah to join them in a military coalition to throw off the Assyrian domination of Palestine which had begun under Tiglath-Pileser III (745–728 B.C.) Ahaz, following the command of God through Isaiah, refused. Rezin and Pekah, fearing a traitor in their midst, then attacked Judah (734) to depose Ahaz. Ahaz promptly (and against God's command this time) appealed to Tiglath-Pileser, who soon attacked Aram-Damascus and Israel. Judah, taking advantage of the situation, then laid plans for a counterattack against Israel. It was at approximately this point that Hosea 5:8–10 was spoken (733).

Foreground. In their drive northward, the Judeans would naturally proceed by the central ridge road from Jerusalem (just south of the border of Benjaminite territory) to Gibeah, Ramah, and Bethel (called

here derogatorily בֵּית אָוֶן Beth-aven, "House of nothing," by Hosea).
The counterattack was successful, and Judah captured not only most
of the territory of Benjamin but also Bethel, on the southern border of
Ephraim. Judah then controlled Bethel through the time of Josiah
(640–609; cf. 2 Kings 23:4, 15–19).

Now you see the reason for God's wrath being poured out
(אֶשְׁפּוֹךְ, v. 10). Judah is in the process of capturing a portion of northern territory, as someone who surreptitiously "moves a boundary
stone" to take some of his neighbor's land (cf. Deut. 27:17). The horns
and alarm are the warnings of war. Benjamin and Ephraim are the
targets. The original attack of Israel and Aram-Damascus on Judah in
734 was wrong. But Judah's vengeful counterattack in 733 was also
wrong. Isaiah (7:1–9) had condemned the former. Hosea here con-
demns the latter.

4. Literary Context

The analysis of literary context has different interests from historical analysis. It is concerned not with the entire historical context from
whatever sources it may be learned, but with the particular way that
an inspired author or editor has placed a passage within an entire
block of literature. Often the most important literary context for a
passage will be the book in which the passage itself is found. How
the passage fits within that book—what it contributes to the entire
flow of that book and what the structure of that book contributes to
it—constitutes a paramount interest of the literary context step in
exegesis.

4.1. Examining literary function:
How a chapter fits a book: Lamentations 5

You read through Lamentations rapidly and begin to notice
how the book is organized. Consulting an OT introduction (4.11.3) or
a Bible dictionary article (4.11.5) on Lamentations, you confirm your
initial observation: Each of the first four chapters is a separate lament
poem organized to one degree or another on the format of an acrostic.

You find that in chap. 1 each verse contains three poetic couplets,
and the first couplet of each verse starts with a successive letter of the

Hebrew alphabet: אֵיכָה (1:1); בָּכוֹ (1:2); גָּלְתָה (1:3); etc. There are twenty-two verses in chap. 1, corresponding to the twenty-two letters in the Hebrew alphabet. You find that chap. 2 is organized similarly. In chap. 3, however, you see a triple acrostic format. In groups of three, the sixty-six verses have at the outset of their couplets the same successive Hebrew letter: אֲנִי, אוֹתִי, אַךְ in 3:1, 2, 3; בְּלָה, בָּנָה, בְּמַחֲשַׁכִּים in 3:4, 5, 6; גָּדַר, גַּם, גָּדַר in 3:7, 8, 9; etc. This third poem doesn't look to you any longer than the preceding two, and you therefore conclude that the different versification is not a real issue. It is the "intensity" of this poem that intrigues you: Will the poet get any more acrostic than this?

A glance at chap. 4 provides the answer. You are back to twenty-two verses again, and the verses are only singly acrostic (בְּ, 4:1; אֵיכָה, בְּנֵי, 4:2; גַּם, 4:3; etc.). And there are only two couplets per verse. Judging from the acrostic and couplet pattern, you see that the book is no longer gathering steam but winding down from the most intense point or climax in chap. 3.

4.2. Examining placement

Turning now to the fifth and final poem (chap. 5), you find a most interesting situation. A single couplet is all that constitutes each verse. Furthermore, these couplets are not arranged acrostically any longer. Only the total number of couplets, as indicated by the verses (22), reflects an acrostic structure—and that only faintly. The relationship of chap. 5 to the rest of the book is now much clearer. It stands at the end of a progression that begins strongly (chaps. 1 and 2), peaks with intensity (chap. 3), and diminishes (chap. 4) to a whimper (chap. 5). Such a progression is one of the classic formats of literature technically called "tragedy."

4.3. Analyzing detail

Even the final verse (v. 22) reflects Jerusalem's tragic state after the Babylonian conquest: Could it be that God has rejected his people, being angry with them עַד־מְאֹד, "completely"? This poignant statement of agonized uncertainty highlights the plight of the survivors.

4.4. Analyzing authorship

Regarding authorship, you conclude tentatively that since chap. 5 integrally relates to the rest of the book it was probably written by the author of chaps. 1–4. Consulting OT introductions, Bible dictionaries, and especially the introductory sections of commentaries on Lamentations, you find conflicting theories on the authorship of Lamentations and/or its various sections. Other steps of the exegesis process (especially historical context, form, structure, and lexical content) are relevant to the authorship question, so it cannot be answered definitively yet. But faced with conflicting scholarly opinion, you must make your own decision. When your own exegesis indicates unity of authorship, you need not avoid so declaring.

5. Form

Knowing the form of a passage invariably pays dividends exegetically. If you can accurately categorize a piece of literature, you can accurately compare it to similar passages and thus appreciate both the ways in which it is typical and the ways in which it is unique. Moreover, the form of a piece of literature is always related in some way to its function.

The example below concentrates especially on this relationship of form and function. In the process it touches on aspects of the analysis of general literary type (1.5.1), specific literary type (1.5.2), subcategories (1.5.3), life setting (1.5.4), and relative completeness of form (1.5.5; 1.5.6).

5.1. Form as a key to function: Jonah 2:3–10 [Eng. 2–9]

In the course of analyzing the literary context of this "Psalm of Jonah," you become aware that there is a question about its placement in the book. Some scholars have considered it an interpolation, inappropriate to its present context. Indeed, some have even suggested that its style is not consistent with the style of the rest of the book, ignoring the fact that style is virtually always a function of genre and form, so that a poetic psalm could hardly fail to reflect a different style from that of the rest of the book, which is narrative. However, to evaluate their arguments effectively and fully, you must determine what type of psalm it is, i.e., its form.

For this purpose you consult a book or commentary that categorizes psalms according to their forms. You happen to choose Bernhard

W. Anderson's *Out of the Depths: The Psalms Speak for Us Today* (3d ed., Westminster John Knox Press, 2000) and from it conclude that the Psalm of Jonah is apparently a "thanksgiving psalm," because it has the five features that Anderson tells you comprise most thanksgiving psalms. They are: (a) an introduction that summarizes the psalmist's testimony (v. 3 [2]); (b) a main section describing the past affliction (vv. 4–7a [3–6a]); (c) an appeal for help (v. 8 [7]); (d) a description of the deliverance (v. 7b [6b]); (e) a conclusion in which God's grace is praised and the psalmist promises to demonstrate appreciation to God (vv. 9–10 [8–9]). Thanksgiving psalms, you note, are prayers of gratitude for rescue from a misery now past.

This sets you to thinking. You had always assumed—perhaps even been told—that Jonah's being swallowed by the fish was a *punishment*. But Jonah is praying a psalm that thanks God for deliverance! Rereading the story, you realize that Jonah's punishment actually came through the storm and being thrown overboard (Jonah 1:12–15). The fish therefore represents rescue from that punishment. Now some things begin to fall into place. The psalm serves the purposes of the story by vividly demonstrating Jonah's inconsistency. In it he eloquently expresses thanks to Yahweh for his own deliverance though he is fully deserving of death; he later resents Yahweh's deliverance of the Ninevites, however, and continues to wish death for them (chap. 4). Knowing the form of the psalm actually makes possible a fuller appreciation of Jonah's character.

A note on the life setting of Jonah 2:3–10 [2–9]: Some scholars have theorized that thanksgiving psalms had their life setting in temple worship. An Israelite would bring an offering to the Temple, recite (or listen to) a thanksgiving psalm while making the offering, and then depart, having pledged to return again to offer other sacrifices. The evidence, however, suggests that psalms were prayed on many occasions in the life of believers (cf. the superscriptions, even though many are surely secondary; the use of psalms by the prophets; and the singing of psalms in non-Temple contexts in the NT, as in Mark 14:26 or Acts 16:25; cf. Eph. 5:19; Col. 3:16). Accordingly, Jonah's use of a thanksgiving psalm was really quite typical. The life setting of such psalms could be any occasion of appreciation for deliverance from distress.

6. Structure

To understand the structure of a passage is to appreciate the flow
of content designed into the passage by the mind of the author, con-
sciously or even unconsciously. But beyond this, it is important to
appreciate the fact that meaning is conveyed by more than just words
and sentences. *How* the words and sentences relate to one another
and *where* they occur within the passage can have a profound impact
on its comprehension. Indeed, structure is often the main criterion for
deciding whether a block of material is a single passage or a group of
independent passages. A key word in structural analysis is "patterns." Patterns indicate emphases and relationships, and emphases
and relationships prioritize meaning. The basic question you must
answer in analyzing a passage's structure is: What can I learn from
the way this is put together? Surprisingly often, by careful work one
can learn more than meets the eye at first glance.

6.1. Analyzing structure and unity: Amos 5:1–17

While working on Amos 5 you realize that it is not immediately
obvious whether vv. 1–17 are a unified whole. You note that scholars
have usually attributed virtually all this material to Amos, but some
have suggested that these verses are a compendium of smaller units
of discourse preached by Amos at various times and places. Following the directions of 1.6, you carefully outline the passage, looking for
patterns, analyzing the poetic parallelism. You observe some interesting correspondences.

Verses 1–3 speak of lamentation (קִינָה) and predict doom for Israel.
Verses 16–17 are similar, with their emphasis on wailing (מִסְפֵּד),
mourning (אֵבֶל), etc. Indeed, vv. 16–17 seem almost to describe the
grief resulting from the destruction portrayed in vv. 1–3. Moving to
vv. 4–6 you note that they have as their theme seeking (דִּרְשׁוּנִי) Yahweh
and living (וִחְיוּ) by avoiding forbidden evil practices. Interestingly, vv.
14–15 employ some of the same vocabulary and likewise contrast
doing Yahweh's will with doing that which is evil. Could there be
other correspondences? In v. 7, the topic is injustice: things being the
opposite of what they should be. Looking ahead, you find that vv.
10–13 share this theme. There, Yahweh excoriates in some detail the
injustices that the Israelites are practicing in Amos's day. In v. 13, רָעָה

עֵת ("bad time") certainly sums up what vv. 7 and 10–13 describe in common. Only vv. 8 and 9 are left. How do they compare? You see that v. 8 describes the fact that Yahweh's power to create means that he also has the power to destroy. And v. 9 also speaks of that destruction, even of the strong (עָז). Finally, you note that in *BHS* the two words יְהוָה שְׁמוֹ at the end of v. 8 are placed on a line by themselves. Apparently the *BHS* editor of Amos (Elliger) is advising you that these two words stand out as having no parallel. Since these words ("Yahweh is his name") are about at the center of the passage, you decide to see if you might structure the passage around them symmetrically. Here is the result:

```
1–3
        4–6
              7
                    8a–c
                              8d      (יְהוָה שְׁמוֹ)
                    9
              10–13
        14–15
16–17
```

This you recognize as a large-scale chiasm, a purposeful concentric literary format. Judging that Amos intentionally structured his revelation in this manner, you reasonably conclude that the passage is unified.

Using the procedures described later in step 11, you would find that J. DeWaard largely confirms your analysis and provides a careful, detailed description of the structure of this passage in an article in *Vetus Testamentum* 27 (1977), pp. 170–77, titled "The Chiastic Structure of Amos v 1–17." You could then use DeWaard's article to refine and adjust your own conclusions where necessary. But you would not need to begin with DeWaard's analysis to discover the basic structural features. That you can, with care, do for yourself. Moreover, having done the basic structure analysis yourself, you are in a far better position both to evaluate and to appreciate the contribution to your exegesis made by DeWaard's article. In other words, the careful exegete is invariably a better "consumer" of what he or she finds suggested in the secondary literature on a passage than the person who turns first to the secondary literature without having done the necessary critical analysis by which the secondary literature can be assessed and exploited most effectively.

7. Grammatical Data

Here is where all those hours spent learning your Hebrew grammar can finally pay off. The goal of grammar is accuracy. In any language, bad grammar may offend our tastes, but its greater danger is that it may block our comprehension. In the exegesis process, a failure to appreciate the grammar in an OT passage is not simply a failure to observe niceties of speech; it is a failure to be sure that you know exactly what was or was not said.

7.1. Identifying grammatical ambiguity: Judges 19:25

וַיַּחֲזֵק הָאִישׁ בְּפִילַגְשׁוֹ וַיֹּצֵא אֲלֵיהֶם

so the man seized his concubine, and brought her out to them

Exegeting Judges 19, you become aware of a puzzling apparent inconsistency. The Levite seems rather inconsiderate (v. 28) of what he has put his concubine through in giving her over to a gang of rapists (vv. 22–25), and yet later he seems so furious at what they (predictably) have done to her that he calls all Israel to war over the matter (vv. 29–30; chap. 20). Carefully, with an eye toward precise grammar, you reread the relevant portions to determine if your initial impression has been accurate. Your special interest is in understanding exactly who the parties involved in v. 25 were.

You note that each of the characters in the story is referred to in more than one way. Specifically, the Levite is referred to as אִישׁ לֵוִי ("Levite," v. 1); אִישָׁהּ ("her husband," v. 3); חֲתָנוֹ ("his son-in-law," vv. 5, 9); and הָאִישׁ ("the man," vv. 7, 9, 17, 22, 28, etc.). The Ephraimite man in whose house he stayed at Gibeah is called אִישׁ זָקֵן ("an old man," v. 16); הָאִישׁ ("the man," vv. 16, 22, 23, 26); and הָאִישׁ הַזָּקֵן ("the old man," vv. 17, 20, etc.). You see from a quick comparison that either the Levite or the old man can be referred to as simply הָאִישׁ ("the man"). Who then is the actual grammatical referent for הָאִישׁ ("the man") in v. 25? The concubine's identity is rather clear, but הָאִישׁ ("the man") is apparently ambiguous. Deciding requires weighing the evidence on two fronts.

First, you note that outside of v. 25, both the Levite and the old man may be called strictly הָאִישׁ ("the man") or may be called הָאִישׁ ("the man . . .") with a modifier, as in הָאִישׁ הָאֹרֵחַ ("the man who was traveling," v. 17) or הָאִישׁ בַּעַל הַבַּיִת ("the man who owned the house," v. 22). Thus הָאִישׁ ("the man") in v. 25 is truly ambiguous. The lack of a modifier makes it so.

Second, you note that in vv. 22–25 it is clearly established that the owner of the house was in conversation with the rapists, but there is no indication that the Levite was. You then decide, rightly, that הָאִישׁ ("the man") can have as its grammatical referent the old man, not the Levite.

Grammatical analysis of course has its limits. In the instance of Judges 19, a separate question remains: Wouldn't the Levite know what the old man had done? Grammar can lead to that question but cannot answer it. Its solution is found both in the analysis of the structure of the passage (a typically laconic biblical narrative, the passage omits all but essential details and expects you to realize that the Levite was unaware of the old man's actions) and in the analysis of the historical context (archaeologically, many Israelite houses had their living/sleeping quarters—where the Levite presumably was— in a back room, as far from the courtyard door as possible).

7.2 Identifying grammatical specificity: Hosea 1:2

לֵךְ קַח־לְךָ אֵשֶׁת זְנוּנִים וְיַלְדֵי זְנוּנִים כִּי־זָנֹה תִזְנֶה הָאָרֶץ מֵאַחֲרֵי יְהוָה

> Go marry a woman of prostitution and have children
> of prostitution because the land is completely
> committing prostitution away from Yahweh.

Exegeting Hosea 1, you are immediately confronted with an interpretational question: Did God actually command Hosea to marry a prostitute? Many commentators have answered in the affirmative, often suggesting that Hosea's wife probably turned to prostitution sometime after their marriage, and Hosea, looking back on his past at a later point when he was seeking an analogy for Israel's unfaithfulness to Yahweh, recast the story of his marriage as if he had been commanded to marry a prostitute in the first place. However, these interpreters do not necessarily have Hebrew grammar on their side.

There are only three words for "prostitute" in Hebrew: קְדֵשָׁה ("cult prostitute"), זֹנָה ("common prostitute"), and כֶּלֶב ("male prostitute"). You observe the obvious: None of the three is used here. Instead, a special compound term appears: The word אִשָּׁה for woman or wife is used in what Hebrew grammarians call the "bound form" or, most commonly, the "construct form" in combination with a governing noun in the masculine plural, זְנוּנִים. Checking any Hebrew reference grammar (4.7.1), you are reminded that the masculine plural is the standard way in Hebrew for conveying abstraction—in this case, not "prostitute" but the concept "prostitution," i.e., in theological contexts, the opposite of "faithfulness." Moreover, you find that nouns in the "construct" are often related logically to their governing noun in the manner of "something characterized by" so that אֵשֶׁת זְנוּנִים would tend to mean "a woman characterized by [the abstract concept of] prostitution" rather than "a prostitute." You also observe that Hosea's children are called יַלְדֵי זְנוּנִים, "children of prostitution" in a precisely parallel Hebrew construction, i.e., "children characterized by [the abstract concept of] prostitution" rather than, "children of a prostitute." You note as well that the verse goes on to say that the land (of Israel), זָנֹה תִזְנֶה, "is completely committing prostitution." Finally, the grammars tell you that the preposition employed at the end of the verse, מֵאַחֲרֵי, "away from," is a compound preposition literally meaning "away from after," i.e., "in the other direction from going after [following]" Yahweh.

Thus the same thing is being said about Hosea's wife, about the children that are eventually born to him, and about the land of Israel in general—and in no case is the literal meaning apparently related to actually selling sex. But what, then, is being said? If neither the wife nor the children nor the population of Israel are being called literally "prostitutes," what *is* the charge against them? That question you must answer partly by reference to literary context and biblical context, though still with a keen eye to the Hebrew grammar involved. Looking at the way that the Hebrew root in question, *znh*, is used predominantly elsewhere in Hosea (and other prophetical contexts, especially Ezekiel), you find that it is employed mainly metaphorically, to convey the sense of "ultimate [religious] unfaithfulness" to Yahweh. Returning to Hosea 1:2, you conclude that the verse is conceptually parallel to Isaiah 64:6 or Psalm 14:2–3 (cf. Rom. 3:10–12). It makes the point, in a somewhat hyperbolic manner, that all Israel has abandoned Yahweh's covenant, so that even Hosea's wife and children—no matter whom he marries—will be tainted by the same unfaithfulness that "the land" in general displays.

7.3. Analyzing orthography and morphology

As 1.7.2 states, the analysis of Hebrew orthography or morphology is not a task beginning students can easily undertake. But its value is often inestimable in connection with problem passages, especially where the decisions of the medieval Masoretes about how words were to be understood may be suspect.

Orthographic analysis removes an oddity: Genesis 49:10

לֹא־יָסוּר שֵׁבֶט מִיהוּדָה

וּמְחֹקֵק מִבֵּין רַגְלָיו

עַד כִּי־יָבֹא שִׁילֹה

וְלוֹ יִקְהַת עַמִּים

In the third line, the Hebrew seems to say "until Shiloh comes" or "until he comes to Shiloh." Both meanings, you conclude, are odd, and your reading reveals a general dissatisfaction on the part of translators with the Masoretic vocalization as it stands. In this case a convincing solution will require some ability to appreciate ancient Hebrew orthography (spelling style), which requires a knowledge of Hebrew beyond the beginner level (see 1.7.2).

The problem may involve vocalization, orthography, and even word division. The combination עַד כִּי ("until") seems clear enough. But is there another way to construe יָבֹא שִׁילֹה? Since שִׁילֹה ("Shiloh") is the really odd factor here, you decide to try to re-analyze it. Removing the vowels will remove the medieval Masoretes' possibly incorrect opinion as to vocalization. You now have שׁילה. Can the word be divided? Could a spacing problem have resulted in שׁילה? You divide שׁי from לה. Looking up שׁי, you find that its consonants are those of a normal Hebrew word (שַׁי) meaning "gifts(s), present(s), tribute(s)." But what about לה? Referring to Cross and Freedman's *Early Hebrew Orthography* (4.7.2), you learn that לה was how לוֹ ("to him") was once spelled. Accordingly, שׁילה could be שַׁי לֹה, "tribute to him." Now you look closely at יָבֹא. Again, removing the Masoretic accentuation so as to have a fresh look at vocalization, you get יבא. Cross and Freedman tell you that in early poems like Genesis 49, the original orthography was vowelless and thus quite ambiguous. So the consonants יבא could represent what was later vocalized as יָבֹא ("comes") or יָבִיא ("brings," hiphil) or יוּבָא ("is brought," hophal), etc. The last option catches your attention, because it fits the context so well.

You conclude (with some well-justified second-guessing of the Masoretes whose vocalizations, after all, represent only their opinions about how words were to be construed long after a passage was originally written) that the "Shiloh" line of the poem should read as follows:

עַד כִּי־ יוּבָא שַׁי לֹה

until tribute is brought to him

The fact that this meaning comports perfectly with the following parallel line ("and the obedience of the nations is his") confirms your conclusion.

A check of the relevant literature (step 11) provides welcome support: Prof. W. L. Moran proposed precisely this interpretation, by far the most convincing in the literature, in an article in *Biblica* 39 (1958), pp. 405–25, titled "Genesis 49:10 and Its Use in Ezekiel 21:32."

Note: Some of the same sort of skill necessary to produce a conclusion may be necessary to evaluate a conclusion confidently. Even if it might never have occurred to you to reconstrue Genesis 49:10 as above, choosing among the options that have occurred to others still requires some careful work. Thus your exegetical effort will reward you as an evaluator of scholarship, not just as an author of scholarship. In other words, as your exegetical skills develop, you become a better reader—not just a better writer—of exegetical studies.

8. Lexical Data

Considerable subjectivity is involved in deciding which words and phrases are the most important ones in a passage. That is one reason why this step comes here in the process rather than earlier: You need to be as familiar with your passage as possible before choosing and ranking terms for close study. Let your own curiosity and the knowledge level of your audience guide you. Where necessary, see which words the commentators select to comment on. But be careful here. A commentator who has dwelt on a word in chap. 5 of his or her commentary may not be inclined to belabor it again in chap. 10. Trust your judgment as to what is important. For the frequency of occurrence of a given word in the OT, you can consult almost any computer concordance, or, for example, Even-Shoshan's concordance (4.8.2). For an idea of how much might be said about a term if one wanted to be relatively exhaustive in one's analysis, see, for example, *TDOT* or *TWOT* (4.8.2).

8.1. *The value of looking at key words: 2 Chronicles 13*

Following the instructions in 1.8, you go through the chapter picking out terms that might call for an explanation. At first you choose freely, without concern for how many terms you will end up with. These are the terms you select:

vv. 3, 17	אֶלֶף	"thousand"
vv. 3, 17	אִישׁ בָּחוּר	"able-bodied soldier"
v. 4	הַר צְמָרַיִם	"Mount Zemaraim"
v. 4	כָּל־יִשְׂרָאֵל	"all Israel"
v. 5	מַמְלָכָה	"kingship"
v. 5	לְעוֹלָם	"forever"
v. 5	בְּרִית מֶלַח	"covenant of salt"
v. 6	עֶבֶד שְׁלֹמֹה	"Solomon's servant"
v. 7	רֵקִים	"worthless"
v. 7	בְּלִיַּעַל	"good-for-nothing"
v. 7	רַךְ־לֵבָב	"indecisive"
v. 8	לֵאלֹהִים	"as gods"
v. 9	לְמַלֵּא יָדוֹ	"to consecrate himself"
v. 9	לֹא אֱלֹהִים	"no gods"
v. 10	בַּמְּלָאכֶת	"in the work"
v. 11	הַשֻּׁלְחָן הַטָּהוֹר	"the clean table"
v. 15	וַיָּרִיעוּ	"and they raised the cry"
v. 15, 20	נָגַף	"routed/struck"
v. 18	אֱלֹהֵי אֲבוֹתֵיהֶם	"God of their fathers"
v. 19	(בֵּית־אֵל) וְאֶת־בְּנוֹתֶיהָ	"(Bethel) and its surrounding villages"
v. 22	מִדְרַשׁ הַנָּבִיא עִדּוֹ	"commentary of the prophet Iddo"

How many of these terms you are able to discuss—and to some extent even which ones you will select—depends on the scope of your paper. You try to choose relatively few words for detailed analysis, realizing that terms needing no extensive discussion can be commented on in the translation notes or elsewhere in the exegesis. You choose five terms as requiring substantial discussion. They are:

אֶלֶף "thousand" (vv. 3, 17)

Your reading has informed you that אֶלֶף means "military unit" rather than literally "1,000" and you need to explain the significance of this in your exegesis.

בְּרִית מֶלַח "covenant of salt" (v. 5)

This unusual term, attested already in Numbers 18:19 and attested in concept although not exact wording in Leviticus 2:13 and Ezra 4:14, will certainly shed light on what Abijah thinks of the Davidic-lineage kingship.

לֹא אֱלֹהִים "no gods" (v. 9)

Such a term is bound to be important for the understanding of polytheism/idolatry from the orthodox Judean perspective.

נָגַף "rout, defeat, strike down," etc. (vv. 15, 20)

Most translations render the word differently in v. 15 from v. 20. Understanding its usage can help identify the divine role in the events described.

מִדְרַשׁ הַנָּבִיא עִדּוֹ "commentary of the prophet Iddo" (v. 22)

An understanding of this document would surely contribute to your appreciation of how the Chronicler compiled his history and the audience for whom he was writing.

From this group of five you decide to choose בְּרִית מֶלַח to analyze by a full word study. You must now follow the process described in 4.8.3 for both בְּרִית ("covenant") and מֶלַח ("salt"). Referring also to the theological dictionaries (4.8.4) as well as the larger Bible dictionaries (IDB, ISBE, etc.; cf. 4.11.5), you learn that בְּרִית מֶלַח is a way of saying, in effect, "perpetual covenant" and perhaps even "perpetual royal covenant," because of the role of salt as a preserver/perpetuator (cf. Lev. 2:13) and because of the association of salt with royal covenant meals (cf. Ezra 4:14). Indeed, the richness of this term occasioned a book by H. C. Trumbull titled *The Covenant of Salt* (Charles Scribner's Sons, 1899), which, if available to you, would certainly be worth consulting carefully in the process of your word study.

9. Biblical Context

Often steps 9.1, 9.2, and 9.3 will flow together. Seeing how the passage is used elsewhere in Scripture (if it is—and not all passages are) helps pinpoint the passage's relation to the rest of Scripture, which in turn leads to an appreciation of its import for understanding Scripture.

9.1. Seeing the broader context: Jeremiah 31:31–34

Your first concern is to find out if the passage is quoted or alluded to elsewhere in the Bible. Because actual quotation of one literary work in another literary work is very rare in the ancient Near East prior to the Roman era, you cannot expect to find one part of the Old Testament quoted in another part. But reference by allusion may exist, and the New Testament certainly both quotes from and alludes to the Old. Here two aids will bring your exegesis a long way before you need to turn to commentaries: the "Index of Quotations" (sometimes called "Index of Citations and Allusions") in most Greek New Testaments, and the column or chain Scripture references in a reference Bible.

Starting with the New Testament index, you find the following entries for your passage:

Jer. 31:31 Matt. 26:28; Luke 22:20; 1 Cor. 11:25
   31–34 2 Cor. 3:6; Heb. 8:8–12
   33 2 Cor. 3:3; Heb. 10:16
   33–34 Rom. 11:27; 1 Thess. 4:9
   34 Acts 10:43; Heb. 10:17; 1 John 2:27

Looking each of these up in a Greek (or English) New Testament, you find that the first three (Matt. 26:28; Luke 22:20; 1 Cor. 11:25) all relate to the institution of the Lord's Supper, and all appear to represent genuine allusions to, though not necessarily quotations from, Jeremiah 31:31. From this you are made aware that, among other things, the Lord's Supper constitutes a reminder of the fulfillment of the kind of prophecy that Jeremiah made in 31:31. The fourth reference, 2 Corinthians 3:6, seems to allude to both Jeremiah 31:31 and 31:34, and gives the original prediction a certain depth of interpretation by emphasizing the enormous advantage of a spiritual relationship to God over a purely technical one wherein the keeping of written rules constitutes the essence of righteousness.

The Hebrews 8 reference is a full quote of the entire Jeremiah passage, which demonstrates its major significance (it is one of the longest OT citations in the NT). But beyond this, its use in Hebrews, a book devoted in part to showing the superiority of the New Covenant over the Old, especially emphasizes how the Jeremiah passage implicitly calls attention to the temporary nature of the Sinai covenant.

The use of Jeremiah 31:33 in 2 Cor. 3:3 is another allusion—not a quotation—in which Paul stresses human participation in a living covenant, allowing you to see that he views the prophecy as having to do with a different—more responsive, more vital—way of relating to God. Hebrews 10:16 provides another actual quote, this time with the purpose of emphasizing how Jeremiah's prophecy envisions an era in which God's redemptive action will render unnecessary the Old Covenant's sacrificial order. That is a perspective you certainly want to take note of.

Parts of vv. 33 and 34 of the prophecy appear in Romans 11:27, with reference to the restoration of the nation of Israel. That aspect of Jeremiah's words cannot be ignored (cf. Deut. 4:31). Paul is finding in the New Covenant the true fulfillment of the promises to Israel.

Examining next the listing 1 Thessalonians 4:9, you do not recognize any obvious allusion to any wording from Jeremiah 31:31–34. "Loving one another" seems to you more likely to be an allusion to Leviticus 19:18 or Deuteronomy 10:18, 19 or Proverbs 17:17 or the like than to Jeremiah 31. Is the "Index of Quotations" wrong at this point? Quite possibly, yes. It is clearly a list you must use with caution.

Likewise, only in a most general sense can Acts 10:43 be considered to refer to Jeremiah 31. Forgiveness is a prophetic promise far broader than one text. Hebrews 10:17, however, is certainly a quote from part of Jeremiah 31:34, again with the emphasis on the possibility of sins being forgiven without continual Old Covenant sacrifices being made (cf. Heb. 10:16, above). But 1 John 2:27, the final listing, with its statement "You do not need anyone to teach you," seems to you not a reference to Jeremiah 31:34 at all. Again, the "Index of Quotations" is somewhat misleading, and you conclude that you may dismiss this reference as irrelevant.

Following a Bible column reference or chain reference yields similar results. Some references will be highly useful; some will be erroneous, based on a similarity in wording or topic but on close examination proving to be not an actual quotation or allusion at all. Sorting through the results generated by a computer concordance similarly requires selectivity on your part. Sensible exegetical work will help you distinguish the relevant from the irrelevant and will help you be prepared in advance to evaluate how well the commentators have addressed the issues raised by biblical usage.

But what about finding passages similar or relevant to the one you are working on when the "Index of Quotations" and the reference lists are silent, or when you want to go further than they do? To do this you must rely on your own knowledge of the biblical context and whatever indications you can glean from books, articles, and commentaries that address your passage and/or its themes. But remember, your own judgment must prevail here. What someone else considers "related" may or may not be. It is for you to decide.

Our example concerned a passage from the Old Testament used in the New. For many passages, the "uses" will be limited to other OT contexts. In not a few cases, parallel or relevant passages must be located exclusively on the basis of thematic or vocabulary connections that you must do your best to locate and evaluate. Topical concordances often help (if there is shared vocabulary), but otherwise only by reading the commentaries or articles on your passage, if they exist, will you become aware of how your passage ought to be understood in a wide context.

Note: Books like Elwell's *Topical Analysis of the Bible* or Davis's *Handbook of Basic Bible Texts* (4.9.2) are often helpful both here and in step 10.

10. Theology

If you are a Christian, the Old Testament is your theological heritage, too (Gal. 3:29). What you believe is informed by its content, corrected by its strictures, and stimulated by its teachings. Theology is a big and sometimes complicated enterprise, but it cannot be ignored. How a passage fits within the whole Christian belief system deserves careful attention. From the many individual passages of the Bible we see the picture of what God has specifically revealed; from the whole orb of theology we have proper perspective for appreciating the truths of the individual passage.

10.1. A special perspective on the doctrine of God: Hosea 6:1–3

This brief oracle is one of several promises of restoration distributed throughout Hosea. Among announcements of coming destruction and exile, now and again one finds reminders that Yahweh will never completely and finally destroy his people but will one day restore and bless a remnant rescued from exile.

Examining Hosea 6: 1–3, then, for its relation to Christian theology per se, you first note that its message is not limited to the Old Covenant. (In general, restoration promises encompass the New Covenant.) Its essence seems to be an invitation to (re)acceptance by God of a people, as the language is plural and corporate, not singular and individual. The passage is thus eschatological from the OT perspective and also represents a partly realized eschatology from the NT perspective. Referring to one or more systematic theologies for a sense of the proper categories (4.10.2), you determine that it touches on the doctrine of sin, in that forgiveness is part of the promise; and it touches on the doctrine of the church, in that God's faithfulness to his people as a corporate entity is promised here (cf. Gal. 3:26–29; Eph. 2:11–22), etc. But its most direct theological impact may well be in the area of the doctrine of God (theology proper). You note that the passage focuses throughout on the relation of God's people to *him*. He caused the punishments; he will heal (v. 1). He will revive and restore (v. 2). He, if acknowledged, will show his faithfulness (v. 3). Thus God's consistency, his mercy as over against his judgment, his approachability, etc., are all aspects of the oracle.

You attempt to assess the passage's contribution to your under-standing of theology as specifically as possible. In this case, the pas-sage says nothing entirely unique in terms of its general themes (concepts), but certainly uses somewhat unique language (words and wordings) to make its points. For example, you note in v. 1 that the description of God's punishment via the verbs טָרָף ("tear apart") and יַךְ ("attack"), combined with immediate promises of healing (וְיִרְפָּאֵנוּ) and bandaging (וְיַחְבְּשֵׁנוּ), is a metaphorical description not precisely paralleled elsewhere in the Bible. The language of "two" and "three" days is also especially dramatic but not intended as a hint of the dura-tion between the crucifixion and the resurrection, you rightly con-clude. The idea that Yahweh shows his faithfulness via nature, and is also as reliable as the more stable parts of creation (v. 3), is hardly without analogy in the Scriptures. But combinations of wordings such as נִרְדְּפָה לָדַעַת ("let us pursue the knowledge of") and שַׁחַר ("dawn"), גֶּשֶׁם ("rain") and מַלְקוֹשׁ ("spring rain") provide an analogi-cal description of God's dependability not precisely to be found in other contexts. You conclude, then, that the passage's most significant contribution to Christian theology is its strong reinforcement of the doctrine of the faithfulness of God by particularly dramatic, even stunning wordings, including arresting metaphors and similes.

11. Secondary Literature

You can waste time and energy in exegesis if you miss articles, books, or commentaries relevant to your passage. Using the process outlined here, you can usually locate fairly rapidly most of the rele-vant literature. This process is not exhaustive, but it is a good way to cover a lot of ground rapidly.

a. Look up your passage in all three volumes of Langevin's *Bibli-cal Bibliography* (4.11.1). That will give you a list of most of the books and articles written on your passage from 1930 to 1985.

b. Look up your passage in the annual (October) numbers of *Old Testament Abstracts* (4.11.1) for the years from 1978 to the present.

c. If you have time, you may also choose to look up your passage in the *Elenchus Bibliographicus Biblicus* (4.11.1) for the years it covers. That can sometimes add an item or two to your list, especially before 1930.

d. From Dillard's and Longman's *Introduction* (4.11.3) or Soggin's *Introduction* and/or Eissfeldt's older *Introduction* (4.1.2), and to a lesser extent from Langevin's *Biblical Bibliography* (4.11.1), you can get a good list of commentaries on the book that includes your passage. To bring this list beyond the late 1970s, you will need to check the annual listings in *Old Testament Abstracts* (4.11.1)—especially easy to do if you have the software version.

e. Quickly go through all the articles, books, and commentaries that are available to you, looking for the books and articles mentioned in those places as relevant to your passage. (Remember: Much that is relevant *to* your passage will not have been written directly *on* your passage.) Add these to your list. Especially helpful here are volumes in series like *Hermeneia* and the *Word Biblical Commentary*, because these series instruct their authors to compile relatively complete bibliographical data both on the biblical book and on its individual passages, up to the date of the publication of the volume in question.

f. Even if you can't read the foreign-language books, articles, and commentaries listed in the previous steps, you can still look through those available to you to see if they mention English-language articles and books relevant to your passage. If so, add these to your list as well.

The process described here, while hardly exhaustive, will get you so far so fast that you will have at your disposal a substantial body of helpful literature against which to check the exegetical work you have done so far.

12. Application

Without application, exegesis is only an intellectual exercise. Every step of the process of exegesis should have as its goal right belief and right action. The Scripture fulfills its inspired purpose not merely in entertaining our brains but in affecting our very living. The Bible is so varied that the applications of its various portions will be diverse. But that does not mean that any given application should not be the result of a rigorous, disciplined enterprise. The guidelines of step 12 are designed to help you keep your perception of the implications of a passage as faithful to its legitimate applicability as possible.

12.1. Samplings of an upright life: Job 31

Here Job concludes his "protestation of innocence," a speech form also found in such places as 1 Samuel 12:3–5 and Acts 20:25–35. He admits that if he actually had done various sorts of immoral acts he would be well deserving of divine punishment. But he steadfastly denies having violated God's law and in the course of his denial describes how a decent, moral person ought, and ought not, to act. It is this perspective that interests you. From 1:8, 2:3, and 42:7–8 you are aware that Job's life has been something of a model of behavior, and you want to see what can be learned from his statements about his manner of life.

Analyzing the life issues (1.12.1) mentioned in the passage, you list six that seem clearly comparable to current life issues: sexual propriety (vv. 1–4, 9–12); honesty (vv. 5–8); just dealings with employees (vv. 13–15, 31); generosity toward the needy (vv. 16–23, 29–34); materialism/idolatry, two issues commonly linked in biblical thinking (vv. 24–28); and financial arrangements (vv. 38–40). Some of the six partly overlap with one another, of course, but treating them separately at first tends to help keep the issues clearly in focus.

Since Job 31 does not contain a direct command to the reader to do something, the nature (1.12.2) of the application is that it *informs*. This does not mean that the application is any less urgent or significant, however.

Does the passage speak mainly of faith or of action (1.12.3)? While some elements related to faith (vv. 35–37, for example), the major interest centers on Job's behavior, i.e., *action*.

What about the audience (1.12.4)? Here the answer may vary depending on the specific issue. Everyone has a personal relationship to sexual propriety, so no person or group would be excluded from that life issue. Likewise honesty, generosity toward the needy, and financial arrangements concern everyone. But not everyone has employees. Most people are either employers or employees, but retired persons or children are usually neither. Furthermore, in the modern world many employers are not individuals but corporations. Recognizing these nuances helps make your application as precise as possible.

Job 31 addresses several categories (1.12.5) of application. It is both personal and interpersonal, and it touches social, economic, religious, and financial concerns. Particularly interesting is the inclusion of the reference to idolatrous worship in vv. 24–28 (i.e., worshipping the heavenly bodies as symbols of deities; cf. 2 Kings 21:3 ; 23:5, 11; Zeph. 1:5, etc.) in such a context. This might help remind you that one important aspect of idolatry as a religious system was that it condoned selfishness and materialism, whereas covenant religion did not.

The time focus (1.12.6) you decide, is relatively unlimited. The potential for sin in the areas mentioned by Job certainly continues at the present and will surely continue until the consummation of this age (multiple NT passages would support that conclusion).

Finally, you must attempt to set the limits of application (1.12.7). Your main concern would be to prevent misunderstanding on the part of your audience. The central application of Job 31 is that an upright life must be decent, honest, generous, fair, faithful, unselfish, and nonexploitive. The passage does not suggest, however, that legal oppression of orphans should be punished by amputation of an offender's arm (vv. 21–22), or that a closed front door is evidence of a homeowner's sinfulness (v. 32). Nor are the particular curses Job potentially calls down upon himself as proof of his decency indicated as appropriate or normal modern punishments. And metaphorical expressions such as "My door was always open" are not literal statements of fact. But if the audience for which you are doing your exegesis might not know some or any of this, whatever you can do to prevent misunderstanding of the passage will be a positive contribution to its applicability.

III

SHORT GUIDE
FOR SERMON EXEGESIS

THIS SHORT GUIDE IS INTENDED to provide the pastor with a handy format to follow in doing exegetical work on a passage of Scripture
for the purpose of preaching competently on it. Each section of the
guide contains a suggestion of the approximate time one might wish
to devote to the issues raised in that section. The total time allotted is
somewhat arbitrarily set at about five hours, the minimum that a pastor ought normally to be able to give to the research aspect of sermon
preparation. Depending on the particular passage, the time available
to you in any given week, and the nature of your familiarity with
exegetical resources, you will find that you can make considerable
adjustments in the time allotments. If you are new to exegetical
preaching, you will need to increase the time allotments substantially.

As you become increasingly familiar with the steps and methods,
you may arrive at a point where you can dispense with reference to
the guide itself. This is the intention of this primer—that it should get
you started, not that it should always be needed.

Comment

Most pastors who are theologically trained have been required to
write at least one exegesis paper during their seminary days. Many

have written Old Testament exegesis papers based on the Hebrew text. But few have been shown how to make the transition from the exegetical labor and skills required for a full term paper to those required for a sermon. The term paper necessitates substantial research and writing, is in many ways narrow and technical, and involves the writer in the production of a formal, typed manuscript to be evaluated by a single professor, with special attention to methodological competence and comprehensiveness, including notes and bibliography. The sermon is usually composed in ten hours or less (total), must avoid being excessively narrow or technical, does not require a formal manuscript, and is evaluated by a large and diverse group of listeners who are mostly not scholars and who are much less interested in methodological competence than in the practical results thereof.

Because the format and the audience are so radically different, is it any wonder that pastors find it hard to see the connection between what they were taught in seminary and what they are expected to do in their office and in the pulpit? Is it any wonder, too, that the average Sunday sermon is so often either devoid of exegetical insight or sprinkled with exegetical absurdities that countless congregations across the land long in vain for "simple preaching from the Bible"? The pastor, having long ago abandoned any hope that his or her weekly schedule would allow for all those hours and all that effort to produce the same sort of high-quality exegesis involved in writing the term paper, has nothing to put in its place. As a result, no real exegesis is done at all! The sermon becomes a long string of personal illuminations, anecdotes, truisms, platitudes, and whatever general insights the commentaries may provide.

The latter are usually far removed from the specific comprehension level and practical concerns of the congregation hearing the sermon. This is a great shame, because the pastor stands in the ideal position to make the connection between the insights of scholarly research and the concerns of practical living, but cannot bring the one to bear upon the other. After all, how can the time be found week by week to devote oneself to the extensive research on which a truly exegetical sermon would be based? Both pastor and congregation suffer for want of a method to bridge the gap, a method that is, amazingly enough, almost never taught in the seminaries.

This short guide for sermon exegesis is both an abridged and a blended version of the full guide used for exegesis papers of chapter 1. Although the process of exegesis itself cannot be redefined, the fashion in which it is done can be adjusted considerably. Exegesis for sermon preparation cannot and, fortunately, need not be as exhaustive as that required for a term paper. The fact that it cannot be exhaustive does not mean that it cannot be adequate. The goal of the shorter guide is to help the pastor extract from the passage the essentials pertaining to sound hermeneutics (interpretation) and exposition (explanation and application). The final product, the sermon, can and must be based on research that is reverent and sound in scholarship. The sermon, as an act of obedience and worship, ought not to wrap shoddy scholarship in a cloak of fervency. Let your sermon be exciting, but let it be in every way faithful to God's revelation.

Note: The more familiar you are with the full process described in chapter 1, the more successful will be your use of the shorter process described here. It is not therefore advisable to skip over the one in order to try to profit immediately from the other.

1. Text and Translation
   (Allow approximately one hour)

1.1. Read the passage repeatedly.

Go over the passage out loud, in the Hebrew if possible. (Research shows that oral-aural memory is stored in the human brain differently from visual memory, so reading out loud will speed and enhance the process of becoming comfortable with the content of the passage.) Try to get a feel for the passage as a unit conveying God's word to you and your congregation. Go over the passage out loud in English as well. (Use a modern translation, unless you and your congregation have determined to use the King James Version. In the latter case you must be doubly careful to pay close attention to step 1.4.) Try to become sufficiently familiar with the passage that you can keep its essentials in your head as you carry on through the next five steps. Be on the lookout for the possibility that you may need to adjust somewhat the limits of your passage, since the chapter and verse divisions as we have them are secondary to the composition of the original and are not always reliable guides to the boundaries of true logical units. Check by starting a few verses before the beginning of the passage, and going a few verses past the end. Adjust the limits if necessary (shrink or expand the passage to coincide with more natural boundaries if your sense of the passage so requires). Once satisfied that the passage is properly delimited, and that you have a preliminary feel for its content and the way its words and thoughts flow, proceed to step 1.2.

1.2. Check for significant textual issues.

Refer to the textual annotations in the *Biblia Hebraica Stuttgartensia* (*BHS*)—or, if you are using it, the older Kittel *Biblia Hebraica* (*BH3*)— or at the bottom of the Hebrew page. Look specifically for text variations that would actually affect the meaning of the text for your congregation in the English translation. These are the major textual variants. There is not much point in concerning yourself with the minor variants—those that would not make much difference in the English translation. By referring to one or two of the major technical commentaries that address issues of text and translation (see 4.11.4) you can quickly check to see if you have correctly identified the major variants. Finally, you must evaluate the major variants to see whether any should be adopted, thus altering the "received" text (the Masoretic text as printed in the Hebrew Bible). If you cannot make a decision—often the commentators cannot either—then you may wish to draw this to the attention of your congregation. In this regard, see also steps 1.4 and 1.5.

1.3. Make your own translation.

Try this, even if your Hebrew is weak, dormant, or nonexistent. You can easily check yourself by referring whenever necessary to two or more of the respected modern versions. Avoid referring to the nonliteral paraphrases (even though some are called "versions" or "translations"), since they will tend to confuse you without helping much. They are confusing because they do not usually represent a direct rendering of the Hebrew original and are thus hard to follow. They will not help much because they are useful primarily for skimming large blocks of material to get the gist—rather than for close, careful study where, to some degree, each word (and just the right word) is important. You may also refer for translating help to an interlinear version (see 4.2.2) or any of the computer concordance versions, the most versatile being AcCordance and BibleWorks (4.8.2).

Making your own translation has several benefits. For one thing, it will help you notice things about the passage that you would not notice in reading, even in the original. It is a little like the difference between how much you notice while walking down a street as opposed to what you can see while driving down it. Much of what you begin to notice as you prepare your translation will relate to steps 2–6. For example, you will probably become especially alert to the structure of the passage, its vocabulary, its grammatical features, and some aspects of its theology, since all these are drawn naturally to your attention in the course of translating the words of the passage. Moreover, you are the expert on your congregation. You know its members' vocabulary and educational level(s), the extent of their biblical and theological awareness, etc. Indeed, you are the very person who is uniquely capable of producing a meaningful translation that you can draw upon in whole or in part during your sermon, to ensure that the congregation is really understanding the true force of the word of God as the passage presents it.

1.4. Compile a list of alternatives.

If the passage does contain textual or translational difficulties, your congregation deserves to be informed about them. The congregation can benefit from knowing not just which option you have chosen in a given place in the passage, but what the various options are and why you have chosen one over the other(s). They can then follow some of your reasoning rather than accepting your conclusions merely "on faith." The best way to prepare this for the sermon is by way of a list of alternatives for both the textual and the translational possibilities. Only significant alternatives should be included in each list. You may expect your list to contain at most one or two textual issues, and a few translational issues. In the sermon itself, you can easily work these alternatives into the discussion of what the text says by such introductions as: "Another way to read this verse would be . . ." or "In the original this part of the verse seems to be speaking of . . ." A short summary of why you feel the evidence leads to your choice (or why you feel the evidence is not decisive) can be provided or not, depending on the demands of time.

1.5. Start a sermon use list.

In the same manner as you compiled the list of alternatives mentioned in 1.4 (and perhaps including that list), keep nearby a sheet of paper or an open computer window on which you can record those observations from your exegetical work on the passage that you feel might be worth mentioning in your sermon. This list should include points discovered from all of steps 1–6, and will provide an easy reference as you construct the sermon itself.

What to include? Include the very things that *you* would feel cheated about if you did not know them. They need not be limited to genuine life-changing observations, but they should not be insignificant or arcane either. If something actually helps you appreciate and understand the text in a way that would not otherwise be obvious, then put it down on the mention list.

Maximize at first. Include anything that you feel might deserve to be mentioned because your congregation might profit from knowing it. Later, when you actually write or outline your sermon, you may have to exclude some or most of the items on the mention list, by reason of the press of time and space. This will be especially so if you choose to make your sermon dramatic, artistic, stylized, or the like, thus departing more or less from a rigidly expository format. Moreover, in perspective you'll undoubtedly see that certain items originally included for mention are not so crucial as you first thought. Or, conversely, you may find that you have so much of significance to draw to your congregation's attention that you will need to schedule two sermons on the passage to exposit it properly.

Remember: Your sermon use list is not a sermon outline, any more than a stack of lumber is a house. The list is simply a tentative record of those exegetically derived observations that you initially think your congregation ought perhaps to hear and may indeed benefit from knowing.

2. Literary-Historical Context
(Allow approximately one hour)

2.1. *Examine the background of the passage.*

There is usually considerable overlap between the literary context and the historical context of an Old Testament passage. Nevertheless, it is helpful to attempt to identify whether some feature is *primarily* literary or *primarily* historical. Accordingly, you should first attempt to identify the general literary background of the passage. Refer to OT introductions (see 4.11.3) and commentaries (4.11.4) as necessary. If it is narrative, what preceded it in the narrative? If it is one of a group of stories, which stories came before, and how do they lead up to the passage? If it is a prophetic oracle, which oracles serve to introduce or orient the passage in any way? Try to isolate both the *immediate* background (preceding paragraphs or sections of the book in which the passage occurs) and the *general* background (the relevant OT literary materials from any prior time in OT history).

Proceed in the same manner with the historical background, referring to the OT histories (see 4.3.2) as needed. Look first for the immediate background and then for the overall background. Be sure your congregation has a sense of what happened before—of what related events and forces God superintended that set the stage for the passage. Some passages, of course, do not have much of a discernible historical background. Psalm 23, for example, cannot easily be tied to any specific events in the psalmist's (or Israel's) past. This psalm, however, does have features that are important with regard to its setting (see 2.2).

You cannot expect to be exhaustive in your analysis of the literary-historical background of the passage in the modest time available to you for your sermon preparation. Therefore, you must be selective in two ways. First, concentrate on the highlights. Select those literary features and historical events which seem to you most clearly and obviously important for the congregation to be aware of. Eliminate from consideration aspects of the passage's literary and historical background which if omitted would not materially affect the ability of your congregation to understand or interpret the passage. In other words, you are searching for the essentials—those things that need to be pointed out in order to represent the background of the passage fairly. These must be *representative* rather than comprehensive. Second, summarize. In some cases, you may not be able to spare more than a minute or two of your sermon to discuss the background of a passage. Try, then, to construct a brief summary of the background information that sets the scene for the passage in its immediate and then its overall contexts according to the broad sweep of things.

2.2. Describe the literary-historical setting.

To have described the background (2.1) and the foreground (2.3) of your passage is a major aspect of describing the context, but there is more. You should also be sure your congregation has some sense of the literary setting in terms of placement and function as well as authorship, and the historical setting in terms of social, geographical, and archaeological coordinates, as well as actual chronological coordinates (i.e., the date when the events of the passage took place).

> *Placement and function.* Where does it fit in the section, book, division, Testament, Bible? Is it introductory? Does it wind up something? Is it part of a group of similar passages? Is it pivotal in any way? What sort of a gap would its absence leave? It need not take long to discern this, and it need not take long in a sermon to pass what you have learned on to your congregation in summary form.
>
> *Authorship.* Who wrote it? Is it clearly attributed to someone, or is it anonymous? Is there dispute about the authorship? Does (or would) knowing the authorship make any difference? If the author is known, what else did he or she write? Is the passage typical or atypical of the author's work? Are there known characteristics of the author that help make the passage more comprehensible? To a listener, a passage of Scripture often seems more "real" if its author has been identified and the general character of his or her writing perhaps described just a bit.
>
> *Social setting (including economic and political setting).* What in the life of Israel at this time would help your congregation to appreciate the passage? Does the passage touch on or reflect any social, economic, or political issues, customs, or events that should be mentioned? Under what personal, family, tribal, national, and international conditions and circumstances were the events or ideas of the passage produced?
>
> *Geographical setting.* Where was it written? Where did the events take place? Do these make any difference in understanding the passage?

Would the passage be different if it were written or its events took place elsewhere? How important is the geographical setting—marginally or centrally? If no setting is given, is this fact significant or merely incidental? Many preachers report that the results of this part of the process especially produce the sorts of remarks in a sermon that cause members of a congregation to say that they felt like they were "right there," i.e., able to imagine themselves in something of the same relationship to the biblical material that the original audience presumably was.

Archaeological setting. Consult the Scripture quotation index of one or more of the OT archaeologies (4.3.5), histories, and commentaries. Is there anything specifically available from archaeological research that relates to the passage itself or to its relatively immediate context? If there is, does it provide a helpful perspective in any way?

Date. Wherever possible, give the absolute and relative dates for any event(s) or person(s) in the passage, or for the literary production ("original publication") of the passage. Most churchgoers know few dates. They usually aren't sure whether Ruth comes before or after David, or whether Esther comes before or after Abraham, or in what century to locate any of them. The more often you take the time to explain the dates related to a passage (it need not take very long, after all), the more clear the interrelationships of people, books, and events will become to your congregation. God's revelation to us is a historical one—do not neglect chronology.

2.3. Examine the foreground of the passage.

What follows immediately, both literarily and historically? What comes next in the chapter(s) following? Is it something that relates closely to the passage or not? How does it relate and what help, if any, does it give for understanding the passage? Are there any events known to have taken place soon afterward that may shed light on the passage? Using the OT histories, check to see if there are aspects of Israelite or ancient Near Eastern history that are not covered (or not covered in detail) in the Bible that nevertheless may help show the import of the passage. Does anything occur relatively soon afterward that might be significant for your congregation to know? Even though an event might not be a result of, or affected by, something mentioned in the passage, are there any events that are similar or logically (even if not causally) related? Follow the same process with the longer-range literary and historical foreground. Try to describe what follows in the book, division, Testament, and Bible that may be of genuine relevance to the passage. Do the same for the historical aspect. Don't hesitate to bring matters right up to or beyond current times, if legitimate. (For example, an OT prophecy about the kingdom of God might well include ancient Israel, the current church, and the heavenly, future kingdom.)

In general, you want to avoid talking to your congregation about the passage in isolation, as if there were no Scripture or history surrounding it. To do so is to be unfair to the sweep of the historical revelation; it suggests to your congregation that the Bible is a collection of atomistic fragments not well connected one to another and without much relationship to the passage of time. That is surely not your conception of the Bible, and it should likewise not be the impression that you leave with your parishioners. Try to pay attention to those things (even in summary) that will help them realize that God has provided us with a Bible which can be appreciated for the whole as well as the parts, and that God controls history *now*, thus controlling *our* history with the same loyalty that he showed to his people in OT times.

3. Form and Structure
(Allow approximately one half hour)

3.1. Identify the genre and the form.

Your congregation deserves to know whether the passage is in prose or poetry (or some of both), and whether it is a narrative, a speech, a lament, a hymn, an oracle of woe, an apocalyptic vision, a wisdom saying, etc. These various types (genres) of literature have different identifying features and, more important, must be analyzed with respect to their individual characteristics lest the meaning be lost or obscured. For example, consider the preaching of Jonah, "Yet forty days, and Nineveh will be overthrown!" (Jonah 3:4). Your congregation will likely be puzzled as to why Jonah, the Nineveh hater, should have wanted to avoid preaching such an obviously negative message of doom, unless you explain to them that the possibility of repentance and therefore forgiveness is *implicit* in this warning of delayed punishment ("yet forty days"). The knowledge of the form and its characteristics leads to the knowledge that Jonah is actually, though reluctantly, preaching a message of hope to Nineveh. It is certainly not essential that you identify every form by its technical name, but you should try to be sure that you identify the overall type of literature—the genre (e.g., prophetic) and then the specific form used in the passage (e.g., the warning oracle), since in most cases such an identification will serve to enhance the appreciation and the interpretation of the passage.

3.2. Investigate the life setting of forms where appropriate.

If any discernible links exist between the form(s) used in the passage and real-life situations, identify these for your congregation. The "watchman's song" used to describe the destruction of Babylon from the vantage point of a sentry (Isa. 21:1–10) has its greatest impact when the congregation is reminded that in ancient times the watchman or sentry on the city wall was often the first person to see something coming and thus to announce news of significant events. Since the prophet, too, is Yahweh's announcer of news or events, the imagery of Isaiah's oracle in chap. 21 is especially appropriate. A knowledge of the original life setting from which the form is borrowed for reuse is often crucial to grasping its significance. Explain these factors to your congregation, and the prophetic message can come across to them with much the same force with which it came across to Isaiah's original audience. You do not need to give a detailed form-critical analysis of the text to your congregation, but you should at least go by the principle that they ought to hear anything about the form(s) that would enhance their grasp of the message. To do less is to leave the congregation partly "out of the loop." Where possible, let your congregation in on anything that helps you follow the meaning.

3.3. Look for structural patterns.

Outline the passage, seeking to discover its natural flow or progression. How does it start; how does it proceed; how does it come to an end? How does the structure relate to the meaning? Is the message of the passage (or the impact of the message) at least partly related to the structure? What are the stages of the "logic" of the passage, and what interpretational clues can you discern in its logic? In not a few instances, the outline of the passage can serve virtually as the outline of the sermon itself. In most others, the two ought certainly to inter-relate in some way.

Then look specifically for meaningful patterns. Are there any repetitions of words, resumptions of ideas, sounds, parallelisms, central or pivotal words, associations of words, or other patterns that can help you get a handle on the structure? Look especially for evidence of repetitions and progressions that may help you understand what the passage is emphasizing. How exactly has the inspired writer ordered his or her words and phrases, and why? What is stressed thereby? What is brought full circle to completion? Is there anything especially beautiful or striking in the structure, especially if the passage is a poem? Remember that the structure not only contains the content but is also to some extent *part of* the content. Structures can be quite prominent (as in Genesis 1) or quite unobtrusive (as in some stories of Israelite kings), but they are usually significant.

3.4. Isolate unique features and evaluate their significance.

Form criticism and genre criticism emphasize the typical and universal features that are common to all instances of a given form or broad category of literature. Structure criticism and rhetorical criticism, on the other hand, are concerned more with the unique and the specific in a particular passage. Both are necessary. You need to appreciate a passage for what it shares in common with similar passages, but also for what it alone contains that specially characterizes it, that makes it different. In terms of the general structure, and also in terms of the repetitions and progressive patterns, what do you find in the passage that gives it a distinct flavor—that describes the passage itself on its own terms and according to its own topics and concepts? What particular revelatory content is communicated within and beyond just the general form(s) and genre(s) which the passage contains or is part of?

4. Grammatical and Lexical Data
(Allow approximately 50 minutes)

4.1. *Note any grammar that is unusual, ambiguous, or otherwise important.*

Your primary interest is to isolate grammatical features that might have some effect on the interpretation of the passage. Anything that can be explained—at least in some general way—is fair game for the congregation. But do not address yourself to minutiae. Find the major, significant anomalies, ambiguities, and cruxes (features crucial for interpretation), if any. Few passages contain many of these, so the task should not take long.

Ambiguities deserve special explanation. If a prophet reports that Yahweh has a word עַל־יְרוּשָׁלַ͏ִם, for example, your congregation will profit from knowing this can mean "about Jerusalem," "on behalf of Jerusalem," or "against Jerusalem." The translations must choose one of these options—they cannot include all three, and thus cannot accurately represent the ambiguity in the passage, which in many cases is a purposeful, suspenseful ambiguity. The audience of the ancient prophet could not always tell whether Yahweh's word was good or bad until the prophet ended the suspense by further words. Cruxes certainly deserve special attention: If the interpretation of the passage (or a doctrine mentioned by the passage) depends on taking some grammatical feature a certain way (e.g., "You shall have no other gods *before me*"), this should be explained clearly. For example, only confusion can result if the hearer remains uncertain about the proper interpretation of this commandment in terms of whether or not "before me" refers to the spatial ("in my presence") or the temporal ("earlier than me") or the devotional ("above me in importance") or whether the use of "gods"—a plural, after all—might imply actual polytheism. People need to know that אֱלֹהִים, "gods," had a range of meaning that included "false gods," "idols," "supernatural beings such as angels," etc.

4.2. *Make a list of the key terms.*

As you go through the passage, write down all the English words (sometimes phrases) that you consider important. These may include verbs, adjectives, nouns, proper nouns, etc. Include anything that you are not sure that a majority of your congregation could define, as well as any terms they might want to know about. A typical passage of ten or fifteen verses might yield a dozen words or more. In the example at 2.8.1, the story of Abijah's speech and battle against Jeroboam in 2 Chronicles 13 yields more than twenty key words and phrases that the average congregation might either know relatively little about or might benefit from having exposited to them (Abijah, thousand, Mount Zemaraim, all Israel, covenant of salt, servant of Solomon, consecrate, no gods, burnt offerings, showbread, God of their fathers, etc.).

4.3. Pare down the list to manageable size.

Because of the demands of time, you must be selective. Decide whether you can include five, ten, or perhaps more of the key terms in your inclusion list. Retain the terms that you are sure your congregation needs to learn about. (From the sample list above, this might include: "covenant of salt," "consecrate," "no gods," "God of their fathers," etc.) Eliminate what is not central to the needs of your sermon, as well as you can predict this. You may find that some important points of your sermon will suggest themselves in the process of deciding what to comment on and what to leave alone with minimal or no comment. From the sample passage above, for example, you might pick "A Covenant of Salt" as your sermon title. That ought to arouse at least a little advance curiosity about the sermon.

4.4. Do a mini word study (concept study) of at least one word or term.

Any sensibly chosen passage will contain at least one important word or wording (thus, concept) worthy of investigation beyond the confines of the passage. Force yourself to follow the weekly discipline of picking a word or term and sampling its usage and therefore its range(s) of meaning first in the section, then the book, then the division, then the Testament, then the whole Bible. Use the techniques for word (concept) study described in 4.8.3, but use your time wisely: Check the various contexts in English if you wish; know what to look for by seeking guidance from the lexicons and published word studies. But whatever you do, get beyond the immediate context of the passage. Let your congregation hear something about that word or wording as it is used *throughout* the Bible as best you can summarize the evidence in the short time you have. Again, remember that there is a difference between a word and a concept, and it is the actual concepts of the passage that convey its message, not so much its individual words as isolated units of speech.

5. Biblical and Theological Context
   (Allow approximately 50 minutes)

5.1. Analyze use of the passage elsewhere in Scripture.

Evaluate those cases where any part of the passage is quoted elsewhere in the Bible. How and why is it quoted? How is it interpreted by the quoter? What does that tell you about the proper interpretation of the passage? The significance of a passage is always elucidated by analysis of the way it is used in another context.

5.2. Analyze the passage's relation to the rest of Scripture.

How does the passage function? What gaps does it fill in? What is it similar or dissimilar to? Is it one of many of similar types, or is it fairly unique? Does anything hinge on it elsewhere? Do other Scriptures help make it comprehensible? How? Where does it fit in the overall structure of biblical revelation? What values does it have for the student of the Bible? In what ways is it important for your congregation?

5.3. Analyze the passage's use in and relation to theology.

To what theological doctrines does the passage add light? What are its theological concerns? Might the passage raise any questions or difficulties about some theological issue or stance that needs an explanation? How major or minor are the theological issues on which the passage touches? Where does the passage seem to fit within the full system of truth contained in Christian theology? How is the passage to be harmonized with the greater theological whole? Are its theological concerns more or less explicit (or implicit)? How can you use the passage to help make your congregation more theologically consistent or, at least, more theologically alert?

6. Application
(Allow approximately one hour)

6.1. List the life issues in the passage.

Make a list of the possible life issues that are mentioned explicitly, referred to implicitly, or logically to be inferred from the passage. There may be only one or two of these, or there may be several. Be inclusive at first. Later you can eliminate those which, upon reflection, you judge to be either less significant or irrelevant.

6.2. Clarify the possible nature and area of application.

Arrange your tentative list (mental or written) according to whether the passage or parts of it are in nature informative or directive, and then whether they deal with the area of faith or the area of action. While these distinctions are both artificial and arbitrary to some degree, they are often helpful. They may lead to more precise and specific applications of the Scripture's teaching for your congregation, and they will help you avoid the vague, general applications that are sometimes no applications at all.

6.3. Identify the audience and categories of application.

Are the life issues of the passage instructive primarily to individuals or primarily to corporate entities, or is there no differentiation? If to individuals, which? Christian or non-Christian? Clergy or lay? Parent or child? Strong or weak? Haughty or humble? If to corporate entities, which? Church? Nation? Clergy? Laity? A profession? A societal structure?

Are the life issues related to or confined to certain categories, such as interpersonal relationships, piety, finances, spirituality, social behavior, family life?

6.4. Establish the time focus and limits of the application.

Decide whether the passage primarily calls for a recognition of something from the past, a present faith or action, or hope for the future; otherwise, perhaps a combination of times is envisioned. Then set the limits. Your congregation would be well served by suggestions of what would be extreme applications, lest they be inclined to take the passage and apply it in ways or areas that are not part of the intentionality of the Scripture. Is there an application that is primary while others are more or less secondary? Does the passage have double applicability as, for example, certain messianic passages do? If so, explain these to your congregation and suggest where *their* responsibilities to respond to the informing and directing nature(s) of the passage lie.

In suggesting applications, it is generally advisable to be cautious. Avoid especially the fallacy of exemplarism (the idea that because someone in the Bible does it, we can or ought to do it, too). This is perhaps the most dangerous and irreverent of all approaches to application since virtually every sort of behavior, stupid and wise, malicious and saintly, is chronicled in the Bible. Yet this monkey-see-monkey-do sort of approach to applying the Scriptures is very widely followed, largely because of the dearth of good pulpit teaching to the contrary. To be cautious involves staying with that which is certain and shying away from the questionable (possible but uncertain) applications. You are not required to suggest to your congregation all the possible ways in which a passage might theoretically be applied. You *are* required to explain the application that is clearly and intentionally the concern of the passage. Unless you are convinced that it is the *intention* of the Scripture that a passage be applied in a certain way, no suggestion as to application can be confidently advanced. It would be far better to admit to your congregation that you have no idea how the passage could be applied to their lives than to invite them to pursue an application devoid of legitimate scriptural authority. In all likelihood, however—if your passage is sensibly chosen and your exegetical work properly done—you will be in a position to suggest in your sermon confidently and practically not only what the passage means but also what it should lead you and your congregation to believe and do.

7. Moving from Exegesis to Sermon

There are many ways to prepare sermons and to deliver them, as well as many different types of sermons and books about them. Still, some general advice can be given about creating a sermon that is exegetically sound.

7.1. Work from your sermon use list.

Organize the various notes on your list into categories. See how many fit together. Do some groups seem especially weighty? For example, does much of the list seem to center on theological terms and themes? If so, perhaps your sermon ought to be especially theological. Does the list contain many elements that are part of a story? If so, might not the sermon take in the whole or the part a story form? Will you need to explain a good many lexical items? If so, perhaps a number of illustrations will be required, and so on. Generally, the material on the sermon use list should at least suggest what some of the major blocks for building the sermon will be, whether or not it suggests a particular format for the sermon. Remember, too, that you probably will not be able to include (or at least cover adequately) in the sermon everything you placed tentatively on the sermon use list. Discard what you must. A single sermon cannot do everything.

7.2. Do not use the twelve- or six-step exegesis outline as the sermon outline.

You will surely not last long in the pastorate if your congregation hears every sermon begin with: "Let us examine the textual problems of the passage . . ." The six-point exegetical outline suggested above provides an orderly and incremental format for covering the exegetical issues of a passage. It is not a sermon outline. You must organize and incorporate the results of your exegesis into the sermon according to an order that has as its primary concern to educate and challenge the congregation. It is up to you to decide what sort of a sermon, containing what elements in what order, will best convey this to the listeners—and no one is in a better position to make such a decision than you are.

7.3. Differentiate between the speculative and the certain.

Let your congregation know which exegetical "discoveries" are possible, which are probable, and which are definite. You may be excited by the possibility that a particular poetic couplet in Hosea seems to be adapted from Amos, but you would be irresponsible to present this as a given, since equally plausible cases can be built that Amos did the borrowing, or that both prophets drew upon a common repertoire of prophetic poetry, or that they were independently inspired with a similar message, etc. There may be no harm in alerting your congregation to any or all of these options as long as you identify them as speculative.

7.4. Differentiate between the central and the peripheral.

The sermon should not give equally high priority to all exegetical issues. The fact that you may have spent a half hour trying to get straight a particularly tricky historical problem of Israelite-Assyrian chronology does not mean that ten percent of the sermon should therefore be given over to an explanation of it. You may well choose not to mention it at all. Try to decide what the congregation *needs* to know from the sermon passage, as opposed to what you needed to know to prepare the sermon. There is much they can do without. Your two best criteria for making this decision are the passage itself and your own reactions to it. What the passage treats as significant is probably what the sermon should treat as significant; what you feel is most helpful and important to you personally is probably what the congregation will find most helpful and important to them. Every passage properly identified is about something—it has a main subject. If your preaching was faithful to the passage, your congregation should be able to go away from church able to state what the "big idea" of the passage was. And by all means, that "big idea" should be something that helps them understand God and their relationship to him, or you didn't think through the exegesis and its culmination in application as carefully as you should have.

7.5. Trust the homiletical commentaries only so far.

Most pastors rely far too heavily on the so-called homiletical commentaries (those which emphasize suggestions for preaching) and not enough on their own scholarly exegesis. This can be counterproductive, since the homiletical commentaries are for the most part exegetically shallow. In addition, since the commentator has no personal knowledge of you and your congregation, he or she cannot possibly provide other than all-purpose observations and insights. The commentator can hardly speak to the controversies, the special strengths and weaknesses, the hot topics, the ethnic, familial, social, economic, political, educational, interpersonal, and other concerns that constitute the particular spiritual challenges for you and your congregation. The commentator has no idea how much or how little your congregation knows about a given topic or passage, how much ground you intend to cover in your sermon, or even the size of the units of the passage you have chosen to preach on. Accordingly, you are advised to refer to homiletical commentaries for the supplemental insights they may offer you after, not before, you have done the basic work yourself.

7.6. Remember that application is the ultimate concern of a sermon.

A sermon is a presentation designed to apply the word of God to the lives of people. Without application, a talk is not a sermon; it may be a lecture, a lesson, or the like, but it is not a sermon. Be sure that you construct a sermon that provides to your people an absolutely clear, practicable, and exegetically based application. This does not mean that most of the time given to the sermon must be spent on the application. The major proportion of time, in fact, may be spent on matters that are not strictly applicational, as long as they help lay the ground for the application. Indeed, you can hardly expect your congregation to accept your suggested application of a passage solely on your own authority. They need to be shown how the application is based on a proper comprehension of the passage's meaning, and they will probably not take the application to heart unless this is clear to them. Likewise, you must not merely explain to them what it *says* while avoiding what it *demands*. The Bible is not an end in itself—it is a means to the end of loving God with one's whole heart and loving one's neighbor as oneself. That is what the law and the prophets are all about.

Reference to the secondary literature is always necessary. There are too many specialized issues and sources for interpreting those issues for the student (or the professional scholar, for that matter) to rely only on his or her personal methodology. To properly interpret a portion of the book of Job, for example, one must have some understanding of the special ways in which Canaanite myths are used, reused (albeit "sanitized"), and otherwise employed in the service of the message of Yahweh's sovereignty over all creation. Likewise, some aspects of the special (old Edomite) dialect used in Job is simply beyond the ken of the seminary student whose only Semitic language is standard Hebrew. One must of necessity turn to the specialists for help, and often even for an awareness of what the exegetical issues are. No one's work may be accepted uncritically, however. Specialists display poor judgment and a willingness to accept unlikely conclusions as often as anyone else. They are capable of giving plausibility to their poor judgments and unlikely conclusions by surrounding them with large amounts of related data and erudite verbiage. Nevertheless, your own common sense and your right to remain unconvinced, until such time as you are shown facts and arguments that seem to you convincing, will serve you well. Your main concern when facing difficult, specialized issues that require expertise beyond your own is not to *originate*, but to *evaluate*. Look critically at what the specialists are saying, compare their logic and their data, and choose from among them what seems most convincing. No one can ever ask more of you.

IV

EXEGESIS AIDS AND RESOURCES

THE HELPS AND BIBLIOGRAPHICAL REFERRALS in this chapter are arranged according to the outline for the full guide in chapter 1. With a few necessary exceptions, the books recommended are limited to those available in English. The best books, in terms of relevancy as well as technical expertise, are listed, regardless of theological slant. However, in the case of OT and Christian theologies (section 10), some attention is paid to differing theological viewpoints.

1. Textual Criticism

1.1. The need for textual criticism

Many pastors and students find textual criticism boring and cannot imagine that it could be more than marginally significant to biblical studies. Boring it may sometimes be—so are many important and necessary scholarly tasks. However, the proper selection of textual readings may be quite significant to the interpretation of a passage, and cannot therefore be avoided. Even those OT books that are relatively free from textual problems—the Pentateuch, Judges, Esther, Jonah, Amos, etc.—still present the reader with textual choices in virtually every chapter. And those books well known for their frequent textual corruptions—Hosea, Ezekiel, Samuel-Kings, Psalms, Job, Zechariah, etc.—can often require of the exegete textual decisions affecting the interpretation of a majority of the verses in a given passage! The task of textual criticism may seem unappealing, even annoying; but it is unavoidable.

There is no single authoritative version of the Old Testament text in existence. The Hebrew text printed in both the older *BH3* and the current standard, *BHS* (see 4.1.5), is merely an edited arrangement of the Leningrad Codex, a manuscript from the early eleventh century A.D., one manuscript among many from ancient and medieval times. Because the formats of *BH3* and *BHS* provide for the printing of this manuscript in full with a selection of alternative readings (wordings) given in the footnotes, the impression is given that the readings in the footnotes are somehow irregularities, i.e., minor deviations from the norm or standard given in the full, printed text. This is simply not so. The alternative readings (called variants) are themselves only a selection of the possible different readings from a great variety of ancient manuscripts of the Old Testament in various languages, each of which was considered both authoritative and "standard" by some community of faith at some time in the past. The choice to print one particular eleventh-century manuscript by reason of its good state of preservation and relatively early date is not wrong—but it can be misleading. If a slightly earlier medieval manuscript had been in the same good state of preservation, it would have been chosen for printing, even though its readings might be different at many hundreds of places throughout the OT. In other words, the variants given in the footnotes of *BH3* and *BHS*, along with the many other variants not mentioned by the rather selective editors of those editions, should be accorded fair consideration along with the Leningrad Codex. Many times, perhaps even a majority of times, they are more likely to preserve the original Hebrew wordings than the Leningrad Codex is. The variants represent many other ancient copies of the OT that may also reflect the original text. In any given instance (at any given point in the OT text), any one of them could be right and all the others that differ could be wrong. Each case must therefore be decided on its own merits even if, as is well known, certain copies and versions are considered generally less reliable than others.

There are many differences between the various versions and

many obvious corruptions (ungrammatical, illogical, or unintelligible wordings) within given manuscript traditions or "recensions." Moreover, outnumbering the obvious corruptions are the "hidden" corruptions—those which subsequent copyists reworked into wordings that seem on their surface faultless but are shown to be unoriginal when the full information from a variety of versions is compared and analyzed.

Because textual criticism can be fairly complicated, and because decisions about original wordings are often subjective, you may be tempted to say: "I won't make any decisions at all about the text. I'll work exclusively from my *BHS* Hebrew Bible." In so doing, however, you will have made thousands of decisions automatically. You will have everywhere in the OT chosen the Masoretic readings of the Leningrad Codex, some of which are best, but some of which are the very worst. You will commit yourself to trying to interpret garbled and incoherent sentences and verses—easily clarifiable by reference to the other versions. And you will, at least tacitly, insult the intelligence of the original human author, as well as the Holy Spirit's inspiration of the text, by accepting uncritically the sometimes nonsensical, sometimes too short, sometimes too long MT when fruitful, helpful alternative readings are available if you are willing to expend the necessary labor to look them up and evaluate them. By the way, doing textual criticism not only sharpens your knowledge of Hebrew, Greek, and any other relevant languages you may read, it also helps involve you in the basic exegetical decisions about the text. A "likely" reading is decided partly by appeal to the general nature, structure, vocabulary, and theological message of the text, i.e., to the other steps of the exegesis process. So doing your textual criticism thoroughly will actually help you do the rest of your exegesis well. To decide against doing any textual criticism is to decide already that certain exegetical issues are beyond you—to give up the fight, as it were, before you start.

1.2. Explanations

If the whole concept of textual criticism is new to you, a good place to get a brief overview of the issues is either:

Emmanuel Tov, "Textual Criticism (OT)" in the *Anchor Bible Dictionary*, Vol. 4, pp. 393–412 (Doubleday, 1992) or

> Bruce K. Waltke, "The Textual Criticism of the Old Testament," in the *Expositor's Bible Commentary*, Vol. 1, pp. 211–28 (Zondervan Publishing House, 1979)

A slightly less readable, but equally comprehensive introduction is found in:

> S. K. Soderlund, "Text and MSS of the OT" in the *International Standard Bible Encylclopedia*, Vol. 4, pp. 798–814 (Wm. B. Eerdmans, 1988)

To begin to learn the method, however, the clearest, most step-by-step introduction to OT textual criticism is found in the following textbook:

> Ellis R. Brotzman, *Old Testament Textual Criticism: A Practical Introduction* (Baker Book House, 1994)

Another erudite, technically excellent volume on the subject that is comprehensible to the beginner, and yet valuable to someone who already knows the subject to some degree, is:

> Emmanuel Tov, *Textual Criticism of the Hebrew Bible* (Fortress Press, 1992)

Also helpful is:

> P. Kyle McCarter, Jr., *Textual Criticism: Recovering the Text of the Hebrew Bible* in Guides to Biblical Scholarship (Fortress Press, 1986)

A classic introduction to the subject is found in:

> Ernst Würthwein, *The Text of the Old Testament*, rev. ed. (Wm. B. Eerdmans, 1995)

This book emphasizes texts and versions but is not terribly useful for actually learning how to do textual criticism.

The Masorah is the medieval Jewish repository of text notes on the Hebrew Bible. Most of these Masorah notes are statistical (a typical note, for example, might say how many times a given word occurs in the masculine plural in Ezekiel) and therefore not terribly useful in modern times when computer concordances can generate the same data—and more—even more quickly. Nevertheless, a student may wish from time to time to understand what a particular Masorah note, as printed, say, in the *BHS* (which has extensive Masoretic notations) is all about. The best introduction to how the Masorah works is:

> Page H. Kelley, Daniel S. Mynatt, and Timothy G. Crawford, *The Masorah of Biblia Hebraica Stuttgartensia* (Wm. B. Eerdmans, 1998)

The complete, classic reference work on the Masorah is:

> Christian D. Ginsburg, *The Massorah*, 4 vols. repr. (KTAV, 1975)

Still helpful for its definitions and explanations on texts and versions and their relevance to OT textual criticism (but not so much on the method of textual criticism itself) is:

> Frederick W. Danker, *Multipurpose Tools for Bible Study*, rev. ed. (Fortress Press, 1993)

If you can find it, a convenient and remarkably thorough source of information on texts and versions, with attention to the individual books, is found in part 5 of Eissfeldt's *The Old Testament: An Introduction*. Its special value lies in the copious references to books and articles on the various topics up to 1965:

> Otto Eissfeldt, *The Old Testament: An Introduction* (Harper & Row, 1965)

Also convenient, though considerably more general, is:

> Roland Kenneth Harrison, *Introduction to the Old Testament*, repr. (Prince Press, 1999)

It is fortunate that this work has been reprinted, because it contains in part 4 ("the Old Testament Text and Canon") not only a valuable survey of the history of Hebrew writing but some judicious evaluations of the limits and fruits of textual criticism. Harrison provides along with each book's introduction a brief description of its textual characteristics and notable problems.

For easy access to clear and practical definitions of terms, alphabetically listed, see:

> Richard N. Soulen, *Handbook of Biblical Criticism*, rev. and aug'd ed.
> (John Knox Press, 1985)

or

> Harry J. Harm, "Glossary of Some Terms Used in Old Testament Stud-
> ies," *Notes on Translation* 11.4 (1997), 46–51

Seeing how an expert does textual criticism is one of the best ways to
try to understand the methods involved. One of the best examples of
careful textual criticism applied to a large section of the OT is worth
learning from if you can find it:

> S. R. Driver, *Notes on the Hebrew Text and the Topography of the Books of
> Samuel*, 3d ed. (Clarendon Press, 1913)

1.3. The versions

In addition to the Masoretic Text (MT)—one manuscript of which
is printed in edited form as the basis of the *BHS* and older *BH3*—there
are five other main ancient versions of the OT in four languages.
Listed in descending order of importance they are:

> *The Greek OT*. Usually called the Septuagint (LXX), but represented in
> *BHS* by an old-style [*Fraktur*] letter *G*, this version represents a
> translation from the Hebrew beginning in the late third century B.C.
> Its importance cannot be minimized. On the average, it is just as
> reliable and accurate a witness to the original wording of the OT
> (the "autograph") as the MT is. In many sections of the OT, it is
> more reliable than the MT; in others, less. Largely because the
> Greek language uses vowels and Hebrew does not, the LXX word-
> ings were less ambiguous and the LXX was inherently less likely to
> be marred by textual corruptions than the Hebrew, which went on
> accumulating corruptions (as well as editorial expansions, etc.) for
> many centuries after the LXX was produced. When you undertake
> textual criticism (except in certain sections of the OT which books
> like those listed in 1.2 help you identify), you can usually place the
> LXX side by side with the MT and treat them as equals. Where they
> differ, either may better reflect the original; no automatic decision

about which to choose may be made, but rather you must analyze the data to see which preserves the original more faithfully.

The Qumran scrolls. These are also commonly called the Dead Sea Scrolls, though they are represented by a *Q* in the *BHS* apparatus. In some cases, e.g., Isaiah and Habakkuk, large portions are preserved in a Hebrew text that is pre-Christian and thus many centuries earlier (and in some ways more reliable) than anything previously known. However, for most books only small fragments have been found. Chances are, therefore, that your passage will not have a corresponding Qumran text. If it does, however, you may generally treat the Qumran wording as potentially equal in reliability to the MT wording. During the Qumran era (roughly 100 B.C.–100 A.D.) many Hebrew words were spelled differently than they were spelled in the earlier Persian period (whose spelling [orthographic] conventions were adopted by the rabbis for the Hebrew Bible as we know it). However, these spelling variations give only minor challenges when comparing Qumran to the MT.

The Syriac OT. Called the Peshitta, the Syriac OT is sometimes (but far less often than the LXX) a useful witness to the Hebrew text from which it was translated (and revised) several centuries after Christ. Frequently when it differs from the Hebrew MT, it does so in agreement with the LXX. It is symbolized by a *P* in the *BHS/BH3*.

The Aramaic OT. Called the Targum, and represented in *BHS/BH3* by a *T*, the Aramaic OT is occasionally important as an indication of the original Hebrew, but is often marred by expansionism and a tendency to paraphrase excessively. Like the Syriac Peshitta, it is a relatively late witness.

The Latin OT. Jerome's translation of the Hebrew OT into Latin (A.D. 389 to 405), called the Vulgate (*V* in *BHS/BH3*) is the only ancient Latin translation that has survived in full. Only rarely is it an independent witness to anything other than the MT, since it was produced from a version that we would call essentially an early or proto-MT.

Fortunately, you are not entirely limited to the use of those versions which are in a language you know. All the ancient versions have been translated into English (see 2.2) and if carefully used, those English translations can give a fairly accurate sense of whether the given ancient version supports or differs from the MT. Moreover, much insight on text issues is to be found in the major "critical" (detailed, scholarly) commentaries that pay special attention to textual criticism (such as the *Anchor Bible, Hermeneia,* the *Word Biblical*

Commentary, and the old but very useful *International Critical Commentary*; see 4.11.4). Also, because the majority of crucial data for making intelligent textual decisions are located in the Hebrew and Greek, the languages most likely to be studied during one's seminary training are also the most valuable for textual criticism.

1.4. Critical text editions

The LXX

After being produced, the LXX was copied and recopied many hundreds of times, just as the Hebrew OT was. All this copying over many centuries provided ample opportunity for different readings to develop, both as a result of accidental miscopyings (corruptions) and as expansions and other "editorial" work on the part of scribes. As a result, critical Greek texts have been required. These contain a single fully printed text, copious footnotes indicating the "inner-Greek" variants (those variants which resulted during the process of hand-copying Greek texts without any regard for the original Hebrew), footnotes indicating the revision-produced variants (those variants which were introduced by the conscious harmonizing of a given LXX copy to some Hebrew copy available to and trusted by the reviser), and footnotes giving information from versions in other languages.

Two major multivolume critical editions of the LXX now exist. Each series is incomplete, but the two together largely complement each other so that almost the entire OT is covered:

> Alan E. Brooke, Norman McLean, and Henry St. J. Thackeray, *The Old Testament in Greek* (Cambridge University Press, 1906–1940)

The following books are available in this series: Genesis through 2 Chronicles (following the English order), 1 Esdras, Ezra-Nehemiah, Esther, Judith, Tobit. The other series is:

> *Septuaginta: Vetus Testamentum Graecum Auctoritate Societatis Litter-arum Gottingensis Editum* (Vandenhoeck & Ruprecht, 1931–)

The following books are included in this series:

> Esther; 1, 2, 3 Maccabees; Psalms (Psalmi cum Odis); Wisdom of Solomon (*Sapientia Salomonis*); Sirach (*Sapientia Iesu Filii Sirach*); the

minor prophets (*Duodecim Prophetae*); Isaiah (*Isaias*); Jeremiah (*Jeremias*); Baruch; Lamentations (*Threni*); The Letter of Jeremiah (*Epistula Jeremiae*); Ezekiel; Susanna; Daniel; Bel and the Dragon (*Bel et Draco*)

Both of the above series use Latin as the means of communication, as do *BH3* and *BHS*. Unlike the NT texts, none of the OT critical editions in either Hebrew or Greek produces an eclectic text (a text that is newly composed from the best possible choices from among all the variants). A partial exception is the Göttingen *Septuaginta*, which is marginally eclectic. The production of an eclectic text is thus up to you. Using the aids at your disposal, you are at least not likely to do worse than the existing MT (called sometimes the "received text"), and may well improve upon it.

A very readable, remarkably comprehensive introduction to the Septuagint exists:

Karen H. Jobes and Moisés Silva, *Invitation to the Septuagint* (Baker Academic, 2000)

Jobes and Silva touch upon all the key issues, giving many examples and explaining the relationship of the Septuagint to the other ancient versions.

Also helpful is:

Emmanuel Tov, *The Text-Critical Use of the Septuagint in Biblical Research* (Eisenbrauns, 1981)

If you need to pursue something about the Septuagint in even more detail, one or more of the following three bibliographies—here listed in chronological order—can point you to most of the works published on the LXX through the year 1993:

Sebastian P. Brock, Charles T. Fritsch, and Sidney Jellicoe (eds.), *A Classified Bibliography of the Septuagint* (E. J. Brill, 1973)
Emmanuel Tov, *A Classified Bibliography of Lexical and Grammatical Studies on the Language of the Septuagint* (Academon, 1980)
Cécile Dogniez (ed.), *A Bibliography of the Septuagint: 1970–1993*. Vetus Testamentum Supplement 69 (E. J. Brill, 1995)

The Dead Sea Scrolls

The various texts are published in a variety of sources. Most are so fragmentary as to be useless exegetically. For a good list of the publications up to 1990, see Fitzmyer, *The Dead Sea Scrolls* (4.11.6). A superb photographic reproduction of the two most nearly complete OT texts from Qumran (Isaiah and Habakkuk, the latter being included in an ancient commentary) is found in:

> John C. Trever, *Scrolls from Qumran Cave I from Photographs* (The Albright Institute of Archaeological Research and The Shrine of the Book, 1974)

The authoritative publications of the Qumran materials are found in an ongoing series, published by Oxford University's Clarendon Press, titled *Discoveries in the Judean Desert*. So far nearly thirty volumes have appeared in this series. Virtually any library or Internet search engine will find these for you if you use the series title, *Discoveries in the Judean Desert*. An example of a recent publication is:

> Eugene Ulrich (ed.), *Qumran Cave 4: Psalms to Chronicles*, Discoveries in the Judean Desert XVI (Clarendon Press, 2000)

The Peshitta

A critical edition of the text is gradually under way, and now covers quite a few portions of the OT:

> *The Old Testament in Syriac*, ed. by the Peshitta Institute of Leiden (Brill Academic, 1972)

The most widely available full copy is an uncritical edition, usually obtainable from Bible societies:

> *Vetus Testamentum Syriace et Neosyriace* (Urmia, 1852; repr. Trinitarian Bible Society, 1954)

For other editions, see Eissfeldt's *The Old Testament: An Introduction*, section 120 (see 4.1.2).

The Targum

The standard was:

Alexander Sperber (ed.), *The Bible in Aramaic*, 4 vols. (E. J. Brill, 1959–1973)

Now, however, the newer multivolume *Aramaic Bible* Project already covers most of the OT Targum with fresh translations and notes. Any library or Internet search engine can locate:

The Aramaic Bible, 17 vols. (Liturgical Press, 1988–)

The Vulgate and Vetus Latina

For both the Vulgate and its predecessor, the *Vetus Latina* (Old Latin), there are editions, based in the latter case on those few portions which still survive, such as:

Roger Gryson, *Manuscrits vieux latins* (Herder, 1999)

There are also inexpensive editions of the Vulgate available. Two common ones are:

Alberto Colunga, Laurentio Turrado (eds.), *Biblia Vulgata* (Biblioteca de Autores Cristianos, 1953; repr. 1965)
Biblia Sacra iuxta Vulgatam versionem, 4th ed. (Deutsche Bibelgesellschaft, 1969, 1994)

1.5. The footnotes and other helps in BH3 and BHS

In the older *BH3* (the "Kittel" edition) there are two separate paragraphs of footnotes. The upper paragraph contains information on variants that are thought by the editors to be of relatively minor importance. They are indicated in the text by small Greek letters. The lower paragraph, indicated by small Latin letters, contains what the editors thought was most significant, including suggestions for actual correction of the MT toward a more likely original. Sometimes the editor does nothing more than record the evidence from the various versions and manuscripts, leaving any decision about changing the text up to the reader. At other times, the editor will actually suggest how the MT should be corrected or at least report what a commentator has suggested by way of a change (emendation). The explanations are given in Latin abbreviations. A convenient English key to those abbreviations and to the signs and major versions is found in a valuable little pamphlet:

Prescott Williams, Jr., *An English Key to the Symbols and Latin Words and Abbreviations of Biblia Hebraica* (Württembergische Bibelanstalt, 1969)

In the newer *BHS* (the "Stuttgart" edition), which most people now use, there are also two separate paragraphs but they have different purposes. The upper paragraph, set in very small type, contains notations related to the Masoretic apparatus printed in the margins (see 4.1.6). The lower paragraph combines and updates the kinds of notations that were grouped into two separate paragraphs by the *BH3* editors. In general, the *BHS* textual notes are superior to those of *BH3* but are still neither exhaustive nor always definitive. They tend to be partial, selective, and occasionally even misleading, so must be used with proper caution. In other words, they are a good starting point, but may not provide all the information you need to analyze the state of the text fully.

For *BHS* the standard key to the Latin used in the notes has been:

H. P. Rüger, *An English Key to the Latin Words and Abbreviations and the Symbols of Biblia Hebraica Stuttgartensia* (Biblia-Druck Stuttgart, 1981). This same key, with minor modifications, is printed in its entirety as an appendix to Brotzman's *Old Testament Textual Criticism* (1.2, above)

Similarly useful is the more recent:

William R. Scott, *A Simplified Guide to BHS* (BIBAL Press, 1987)

The latest aid to using the *BHS* is:

Reinhard Wonneberger, *Understanding BHS: A Manual for the Users of Biblia Hebraica Stuttgartensia*, 2d ed. (Pontifical Biblical Institute Press, 1990)

The critical apparatus in both *BH3* and *BHS* will help you see at a glance *some* of the evidence for certain obvious textual issues, but they are no substitute for your own comprehensive word-by-word check of the versions in a full exegetical analysis of a passage.

1.6 The Hebrew University Bible Project and Biblia Hebraica Quinta

Hebrew University Bible Project

Begun in Jerusalem in 1965, this project will eventually produce a massive, multivolume critical edition of the Hebrew OT. However, so far only Isaiah and Jeremiah have been completed, though Ezekiel is scheduled to appear soon—so progress has been slow. This edition is based on the Aleppo Codex, which dates to about 900–925 A.D. (i.e., perhaps as much as a century earlier than the Leningrad Codex). Unfortunately, the Aleppo Codex is incomplete, lacking almost the entire Pentateuch, as well as some or all of Song of Songs, Ecclesiastes, Lamentations, Esther, Daniel, and Ezra. The project will, of course, cover these gaps by using the Leningrad Codex and other ancient MSS as necessary.

The goal of the project is to provide all relevant textual information, and its four (!) apparatuses of text notes and textual commentary really do cover everything textual rather thoroughly. The project has a slightly problematic bias, however: It tends to believe that most textual variations resulted from various translation, transmission, and interpretive *techniques* (theoretically) employed by ancient scribes rather than from *mistakes*, i.e., actual variants produced by miscopying over the years. While most scholars reject this bias, it doesn't hurt your ability to get all the information you want from the apparatuses, because they provide such complete data and such thorough discussions of the evidence. Here are the two fascicles available as of the publication of this guide:

Moshe H. Goshen-Gottstein (ed.), *The Book of Isaiah* (Magnes, 1995)
Shemaryahu Talmon and Emmanuel Tov (eds.), *The Book of Jeremiah* (Magnes, 1998)

Quinta

Just as *BHS* has now almost completely replaced the use of the older *BH3*, a new edition of the Hebrew Bible is under way with the expectation that it will replace *BHS*. This new edition is called *Biblia Hebraica Quinta* (*BH5—BHS* was essentially "*BH4*"), and it is based on the same excellent manuscript as that of its predecessors, the Leningrad Codex of 1008 A.D. The big change with the *Quinta* will be its "apparatus" (notes and commentary). These will distinguish text issues that are based on "external evidence" (other versions) from issues based on "internal evidence" (in the MT tradition itself) and will address questions of the MT's literary development over time. The textual commentary, which will explain how textual choices were made, should be a real improvement over the *BH3* and *BHS*. The first fascicle to appear so far covers only the book of Ruth, but is especially valuable for including a general introduction to the whole project.

As the Hebrew University Bible Project and the *Quinta* progress, they will provide a slow but presumably steady trickle of very valuable text editions and textual data, eventually rendering obsolete even the currently essential *BHS*.

1.7. The Masora

Printed in the margins of both *BH3* and *BHS* are groups of notations—written in Aramaic and mostly abbreviated—made by the Masoretes. Some notations may suggest possible improvements upon the text, but most indicate observations useful to the accurate preservation and copying of the text. In the ancient Masoretic manuscripts, many of these notes were placed in the margins. These were called the *masora parva*, the "little Masora." Longer notations were placed at the beginning or the end of the manuscripts. These were called the *masora magna*, the "large Masora." For most purposes of exegesis, the Masora itself is paid little attention by scholars because its truly significant observations are already incorporated into the notes in *BH3* and *BHS* or can be duplicated by quick reference to a concordance. Moreover, such observations have been rendered unnecessary by the development of the printing press. In other words, it is quite common to ignore the Masora in doing exegesis. You will be in good company to do so.

1.8. Other Masoretic indicators

The Masoretes produced a dots-and-dashes vowel pointing system so that their students, for whom Hebrew was by then a dead language, could pronounce the words properly (i.e., properly according to the postbiblical pronunciation that had evolved by the sixth to ninth centuries A.D.), mainly for the purpose of chanting the text in synagogue worship. In addition, they developed special symbols to indicate word accents, verse divisions, and sections of verses, again mainly for the purpose of group chanting in worship. They also included notations for such things as Scripture portions used in the yearly cycle of synagogue readings. None of these markings or notations, including the vowel pointing system, represents anything more than the opinion of the Masoretes according to their own early medieval, and often conflicting, traditions. In other words, you must be ready to disregard pointings, verse divisions, and other markings whenever your exegetical judgment suggests that they are unreliable. Much more information on the Masoretic indicators is found in 4.1.2.

2. Translation

2.1. Translation theory

A good translation not only renders the words of the original into their best English equivalents, it also reflects the style, the spirit, and even the impact of the original wherever possible. You are the best judge of what constitutes a faithful translation. Your familiarity with the passage in the original, and with the audience for whom you write or preach, allows you to choose your words to maximize the accuracy of the translation. Remember that accuracy does not require wooden literalism. The words of different languages do not correspond to one another on a one-for-one basis. It is the concepts that must correspond. Your translation should leave the same impression with you when you read it as does the original. A translation that meets this criterion can be considered faithful to the original.

Two books on Bible translation remain valuable. Both should be read in their entirety, rather than referred to only for specific information:

Eugene A. Nida and Charles R. Taber, *The Theory and Practice of Translation* (E. J. Brill, 1974)

> John Beekman and John Callow, *Translating the Word of God* (Zondervan Publishing House, 1974)

These books contain discussions of the special problems presented by translating Scripture from one language to another. They provide advice on how to handle metaphors, similes, words with multiple meanings, idioms, etc. Also useful is:

> Sakae Kubo and Walter Specht, *So Many Versions?* (Zondervan Publishing House, 1975)

Kubo and Specht review at length the major twentieth-century translations of the Bible, providing copious examples from each, and commenting throughout on the translation techniques and assumptions involved.

2.2. Translation aids

Even if your knowledge of Hebrew, Greek, and other languages has deteriorated (or was never adequate), you can still work profitably with the original languages by using several English-oriented texts. Don't hesitate to use these. There is no shame in saving time and frustration, and no value in guessing your way through material you simply can't read.

The fastest and most versatile basic translation aids come in the form of computer software, the two most powerful being *AcCordance* and *BibleWorks* (see 8.2). These programs provide instant lexical and grammatical data for any word you point your cursor at. They also can assemble for you in seconds all the various contexts where a given word is used throughout the rest of Scripture so that you can examine for yourself the range of its usages. Moreover, they can instantly provide a complete list of translated contexts in any of the modern translations whose modules you have purchased so that you can readily examine how various modern translators have dealt with your word or wording in various parts of their translations. All this is enormously useful, but it does not automatically render useless the book references listed below. A book can be selective and focused at various points according to the author's judgment in a way that the mechanical processes of a computer concordance do not allow, and a book can also follow a particular format or variety of formats for the presenting of its data (including the unique way that an author may have chosen to show the intersection of his or her specific advice to you within the context of a helpfully formatted text). Moreover, a book can show judiciously selected combinations of contexts that may prove more helpful to you in some instances than the automatic complete screen formats generated by the computer concordances.

For the Hebrew OT several complete interlinear editions are available. Each contains an acceptable translation printed in interlinear fashion, as well as separately in paragraph form alongside the main text. Interlinears can be useful for skimming through larger passages:

Jay P. Green (ed.), *Interlinear Bible: Hebrew, Greek, English* (Sovereign Grace Publishers, 1997)

Jay P. Green (ed.), *Interlinear Bible: Hebrew, Greek, English,* large edition (Sovereign Grace Publishers, 2000)

John R. Kohlenberger, III (ed.), *NIV Interlinear Hebrew-English Old Testament* (Zondervan Publishing House, 1987)

Also available for part of the OT is a similar interlinear edition, somewhat less useful because it is more wooden in style:

Joseph Magil, *The Englishman's Linear Hebrew-English Old Testament* (Zondervan Publishing House, 1974)

For the LXX no interlinear is available, but a convenient side-by-side Greek and English publication does exist:

The Septuagint Version of the Old Testament with an English Translation (Samuel Bagster & Sons, n.d.; repr. Zondervan Publishing House, 1972)

A translation of the Syriac Peshitta into English has been made. It is usually reliable, and serves to tell you when the Peshitta is different from the MT and other versions, even if you do not know Syriac well:

George M. Lamsa, *The Holy Bible from Ancient Eastern Manuscripts* (A. J. Holman Co., 1957)

Various portions of the Aramaic Targums are available in English translation. Among these are:

J. W. Etheridge, *The Targums of Onkelos and Jonathan ben Uzziel on the Pentateuch*, 2 vols. (Longman, Green, Longman & Roberts, 1862–1865; repr. KTAV Publishing House, 1969)

Bernard Grossfeld (ed.), *The Targum to the Five Megilloth* (Hermon Press, 1973)

The Latin Vulgate is also translated into English:

Ronald Knox, *The Old Testament: Newly Translated from the Vulgate Latin*, 2 vols. (Sheed & Ward, 1950)

Analytical lexicons list words directly as they occur in the biblical text, and then provide the parsing. They can be useful as time-savers, or if you have no access to a computer program to do the same thing, but are not be to relied on for meanings or other technical data. Use the formal lexicons for that purpose. For Hebrew and Aramaic there is:

Benjamin Davidson, *The Analytical Hebrew and Chaldee Lexicon* (Samuel Bagster & Sons, 1848; 2d ed. 1850; repr. Zondervan Publishing House, 1970)

For LXX Greek words, Bagster's analytical lexicon of the NT is often adequate even though its vocabulary is limited to words found in the NT:

Harold K. Moulton (ed.), *The Analytical Greek Lexicon Revised* (originally published as *The Analytical Greek Lexicon*, Samuel Bagster & Sons, 1852; rev. ed. 1908; new rev. Zondervan Publishing House, 1978)

To make it easier to use the still-popular Brown, Driver, and Briggs Hebrew Lexicon (see 4.8.1), an index was produced that lists the Hebrew words mostly in the order in which they occur in the chapters and verses of each book, with reference given to the appropriate entry in *BDB*. Of course, such an aid is necessary only if your Hebrew is weak enough to make parsing a problem:

Bruce Einspahr, *Index to the Brown, Driver and Briggs Hebrew Lexicon* (Moody Press, 1976)

You must use a reliable lexicon for careful exegesis. But if you are reading a passage in Hebrew for the first time, or trying to read through several passages quickly—and your Hebrew vocabulary is limited—you will find the following books to be time-savers:

John Joseph Owens, *Analytical Key to the Old Testament* (Baker Book House, 1989)

Terry A. Armstrong, *A Reader's Hebrew-English Lexicon of the Old Testament* (Zondervan Publishing House, 1980)

3. History

3.1. General chronology

Comprehensive overviews of the chronology of the ancient Near East, including Israel, may be found in any of the following works:

William W. Hallo and William K. Simpson, *The Ancient Near East: A History* (Harcourt Brace, 1997)

Amelie Kuhrt, *The Ancient Near East: 3000–330 BC* (Routledge, 1997)

Jack Sasson, *Civilization of the Ancient Near East*, 2 vols. (Hendrickson, 2000)

Donald B. Redford, *Egypt, Canaan and Israel in Ancient Times* (Princeton University Press, 1992)

A convenient, shorter treatment of chronological issues specifically involving Israel is:

Jack Finegan, *Handbook of Biblical Chronology* (Hendrickson, 1998)

The difficult problem of synchronizing the biblical chronologies of the Israelite and Judean kings is well handled by Thiele, whose ingenious solutions have increasingly gained acceptance:

Edwin R. Thiele, The *Mysterious Numbers of the Hebrew Kings*, rev. ed. (Zondervan Publishing House, 1983)

Two alternative approaches with different analyses of some of the more controversial chronological puzzles have also been written:

Gershon Galil, *The Chronology of the Kings of Israel and Judah* (E. J. Brill, 1996)

J. H. Hayes and P. K. Hooker, *A New Chronology for the Kings of Israel and Judah* (John Knox Press, 1988)

3.2. Israelite history

Most histories are written to be studied in their entirety rather than consulted here and there for information about specific times or events. Several major Israelite histories exist, however, which are fairly well suited to both purposes. The first listed, by Kaiser, is especially convenient to use by reason of its indices for subject, author, and Scripture reference, as well as for its extensive glossary and bibliography.

> Walter C. Kaiser, Jr., *A History of Israel: From the Bronze Age to the Jewish Wars* (Broadman and Holman, 1998)
>
> Eugene Merrill, *Kingdom of Priests: A History of Old Testament Israel* (Baker Book House, 1987)
>
> Leon J. Wood, *A Survey of Israel's History* (Zondervan Publishing House, 1986).
>
> J. Maxwell Miller and John H. Hayes, *A History of Ancient Israel and Judah* (Westminster Press, 1986)

Combining both history and a survey of the OT books themselves is the classic work:

> Samuel J. Schultz, with John Loudon (ed.), *The Old Testament Speaks: A Complete Survey of Old Testament History and Literature*, 5th ed. (HarperCollins, 2000)

Still widely used and respected for its cautious, judicious, and thorough scholarship is:

> John Bright, *A History of Israel*, 4th ed. Introduction and Appendix by William P. Brown (Westminster John Knox Press, 2000)

Especially welcome because it follows very closely the Old Testament ordering and subject matter rather than being more generally a "secular" history of Israel is the classic:

> Charles F. Pfeiffer, *Old Testament History* (Baker Book House, 1973)

Somewhat more specialized in focus are:

> Patrick D. Miller, *The Religion of Ancient Israel* (Westminster John Knox Press, 2000)

Rainer Albertz, *A History of Israelite Religion in the Old Testament Period*, 2 vols. (Westminster John Knox Press, 1994)

Readable and erudite, even though edited by a non-academician, is:

Herschel Shanks (ed.), *Ancient Israel: From Abraham to the Roman Destruction of the Temple* (Biblical Archaeology Society, 1999)

The many volumes of the prestigious Cambridge Ancient History series include several that cover issues directly relevant to OT history. For example:

John Boardman (ed.), *The Assyrian and Babylonian Empires and Other States of the Near East, from the Eighth to the Sixth Centuries* (Cambridge University Press, 1992)
John Boardman (ed.), *Persia, Greece, and the Western Mediterranean, 525–479 B.C.* (Cambridge University Press, 1988)

3.3. Israelite and ancient Near Eastern culture

For understanding the Bible in its immediate sociological context, nothing excels the classic:

Roland DeVaux, *Ancient Israel: Its Life and Institutions*, repr. (Eerdmans/Dove, 1997)

Two other volumes with a similar purpose are:

Daniel C. Snell, *Life in the Ancient Near East, 3100–332 B.C.E.* (Yale University Press, 1998)
Michael D. Coogan (ed.), *The Oxford History of the Biblical World* (Oxford University Press, 1998)

These books are paralleled by and in some cases supplemented by:

J. David Pleins, *The Social Visions of the Hebrew Bible* (Westminster John Knox Press, 2000)
Victor H. Matthews and Don C. Benjamin, *The Social World of Ancient Israel* (Hendrickson, 1995)
John H. Walton, Victor H. Matthews, and Mark W. Chavalas, *The IVP Bible Background Commentary: Old Testament* (Intervarsity Press, 2000)

John W. Walton, *Ancient Israelite Literature in Its Cultural Context* (Zondervan Publishing House, 1989)

Wolfram vonSoden, *The Ancient Orient: An Introduction to the Study of the Ancient Near East* (Wm. B. Eerdmans, 1994)

More narrowly focused but comparable in their usefulness relative to the cultural subcategories they address are the following four books:

Moshe Weinfeld, *Social Justice in Ancient Israel and in the Ancient Near East* (Augsburg/Fortress Press, 1995)

H. J. Boecker, *Law and the Administration of Justice in the Old Testament and Ancient East* (Augsburg, 1980)

Herbert G. Livingstone, *The Pentateuch in Its Cultural Environment*, 2d ed. (Baker Book House, 1987)

Norman K. Gottwald, *The Politics of Ancient Israel* (Westminster John Knox Press, 2000)

3.4. Other parts of the ancient Near East

From among the many fine historical works on various peoples and cultures in the biblical world, several major works may be recommended for their comprehensiveness and reliability.

For a general presentation of the data on ethnic and national groups mentioned in the OT as Israel's neighbors or conquerors, see either of the following two volumes:

Alfred J. Hoerth, Gerald L. Mattingly, and Edwin Yamauchi (eds.), *Peoples of the Old Testament World* (Baker Book House, 1998)

Donald J. Wiseman (ed.), *Peoples of Old Testament Times* (Oxford University Press, 1973)

On Egyptian history more than one excellent work is available:

Cyril Aldred, *The Egyptians* (Thames and Hudson, 1998)

Alan Gardiner, *Egypt of the Pharaohs* (Oxford University Press, 1966)

Donald Redford (ed.), *The Oxford Encyclopedia of Ancient Egypt*, 3d ed., 3 vols. (Oxford University Press, 2000)

Some fine volumes have been written that address the parallels and connections between Old Testament and Egyptian history and culture:

John D. Currid, *Ancient Egypt and the Old Testament* (Baker Book House, 1997)

Donald B. Redford, *Egypt, Canaan and Israel in Ancient Times* (Princeton University Press, 1993)

Specifically for the culture and religion of the Egyptians, including a sensitive analysis of the Egyptian mythopoeic (myth-making) religious mind, read if you can find it:

Henri Frankfort, *Ancient Egyptian Religion* (Harper & Row, Harper Torchbooks, 1961)

Significant relations between the Israelites and the Assyrians and Babylonians were more or less constant during the years from 745 B.C. to 540 B.C., the time of the production of the vast majority of the prophetical books of the OT as well as the subject of much of the content of Kings and Chronicles. For Assyrian and Babylonian history, see:

H. W. F. Saggs, *The Greatness That Was Babylon: A Survey of the Ancient Civilization of the Tigris-Euphrates Valley*, repr. (St. Martin's Press, 1988)

H. W. F. Saggs, *The Might That Was Assyria*, repr. (St. Martin's Press, 1990)

George Roux, *Ancient Iraq* (Viking Penguin, 1993)

Very helpful specifically for its insights into the time of Nebuchadnezzar the Great is:

Donald J. Wiseman, *Nebuchadnezzar and Babylon* (Oxford University Press, 1991)

A reliable general survey of the literature, life, religion, and civil institutions of the ancient Sumerians, Babylonians, and Assyrians is found in:

A. Leo Oppenheim, *Ancient Mesopotamia*, rev. ed. (University of Chicago Press, 1976)

Increased interest in Sumerian history and culture has resulted from the extraordinary new finds at Syrian Ebla. Two good introductions to Sumerian literature are available, and both contain descriptions of some Sumerian documents with biblical parallels:

Samuel N. Kramer, *The Sumerians* (University of Chicago Press, 1990)
C. Leonard Woolley, *The Sumerians* (W. W. Norton & Co., 1978)

The Hittites exerted considerable early influence on Bible lands, even though they are not specifically mentioned in the Bible. (The "Hittites" of the Bible are the Sons of Heth, a Canaanite subgroup.) The standard introduction to their history and civilization is:

O. R. Gurney, *The Hittites*, 2d ed. (Penguin Books, 1954)

For Persia, three fine histories are available. The first of these is of special note because of its conscious focus on OT connections:

Edwin M. Yamauchi, *Persia and the Bible* (Baker Book House, 1997)
Josef Wiesehofer, *Ancient Persia: From 550 BC to 650 AD* (St. Martin's Press, 1998)
Pierre Briant, *From Cyrus to Alexander: A History of the Persian Empire*, 2 vols. (Eisenbrauns, 2000)

Olmstead's classic history of Persia (with helpful indexes) is still extremely valuable, if you can find it:

A. T. Olmstead, *History of the Persian Empire* (University of Chicago Press, 1948)

For matters related to the Ugaritic civilization, the Phoenicians, the Canaanites, and the Philistines, see the relevant volumes from the following:

Marguerite Yon, *The City of Ugarit at Ras Shamra* (Eisenbrauns, 2000)
Jacob H. Katzenstein, *The History of Tyre*, rev. ed. (Ben Gurion University, 1997)
Jonathan N. Tubb, *Canaanites: Peoples of the Past* (University of Oklahoma Press, 1998)
Trude Dothan and M. Dothan, *People of the Sea: Search for the Philistines* (Macmillan Publishing Co., 1992)
Othniel Margalith, *Sea Peoples in the Bible* (Harrassowitz, 1994)

3.5. Archaeology

Several introductions to the field of Palestinian archaeology are widely used, and a variety of valuable sources are also available for specific knowledge about individual areas and sites. Unfortunately, many archaeologists either do not publish their excavation results at all or publish them in such a narrow, technical way that the average OT student cannot make reasonable use of them in exegesis, except as the excavation reports themselves draw attention to biblical texts. Among the most useful of recent works on biblical archaeology are the following. Any of them may prove useful, depending on the nature of your passage.

> John D. Currid. *Doing Archaeology in the Land of the Bible: A Basic Guide* (Baker Book House, 1999)
>
> Amnon Ben-Tor, *The Archaeology of Ancient Israel* (Yale University Press, 1992)
>
> Brian Fagan (ed.), *The Oxford Companion to Archaeology* (Oxford University Press, 1996)
>
> Alfred J. Hoerth, *Archaeology of the Old Testament* (Baker Book House, 1998)
>
> Amihai Mazar, *Archaeology of the Land of the Bible: 10,000–586 B.C.E.* (Doubleday, 1992)

The following two excellent multivolume dictionaries of archaeology are each quite comprehensive. They are among the sources you would be well advised always to check.

> Eric M. Meyers (ed.), *The Oxford Encyclopedia of Archaeology in the Near East*, 5 vols. (Oxford University Press, 1996)
>
> Ephraim Stern (ed.), *New Encyclopedia of Archaeological Excavations in the Holy Land*, 4 vols. (Israel Exploration Society and Carta; and Simon and Schuster, 1993)

Concentrating on urban archaeology are:

> Volkmar Fritz, *The City in Ancient Israel* (Sheffield Academic Press, 1995)
>
> Lamoine DeVries, *Cities of the Biblical World* (Hendrickson, 1997)

These two books may prove useful to you in terms of their specialized interests:

Thomas E. Levy, *The Archaeology of Society in the Holy Land* (Cassell Academics, 1998)

Israel Finkelstein, *The Archaeology of the Israelite Settlement* (IES, 1988)

Still valuable, from the pens of great Palestinian archaeologists, are:

William F. Albright, *The Archaeology of Palestine*, rev. ed. (Penguin Books, 1954; repr. Peter Smith, 1960)

William F. Albright, *Archaeology and the Religion of Israel*, 4th ed. (Johns Hopkins Press, 1968)

Yohanan Aharoni, *The Archaeology of the Land of Israel* (Westminster Press, 1982)

G. Ernest Wright, *Biblical Archaeology*, rev. ed. (Westminster Press, 1963)

Kathleen Kenyon, *Archaeology in the Holy Land*, 4th ed. (W. W. Norton & Co., 1979)

Kathleen Kenyon, *The Bible and Recent Archaeology* (John Knox Press, 1978)

Michael Avi-Yonah (ed.), *Encyclopedia of Archaeological Excavations in the Holy Land*, 4 vols. (Prentice-Hall, 1975)

Emphasizing inscriptional evidence is the recent:

Kyle P. McCarter, Jr., *Ancient Inscriptions: Voices from the Biblical World* (Biblical Archaeology Society, 1996)

A fine example of archaeology applied to the interpretation of prophetical books is:

Philip J. King, *Amos, Hosea, Micah—An Archaeological Commentary* (Westminster Press, 1988)

For a collection of maps, illustrations, and generally reliable commentary on the relationship of archaeological discoveries to OT history, particularly as related to specific books and even passages, consult:

Gaalyahu Cornfeld, *Archaeology of the Bible: Book by Book*; David Noel Freedman, consulting ed. (Harper & Row, 1976)

Gonzalo Baez-Carmago, *Archaeological Commentary on the Bible* (Doubleday, 1984)

For an extensive review of the actual literary and historical sources of the ancient world from which archaeological information comes, the following remains useful:

D. Winton Thomas (ed.), *Archaeology and Old Testament Study* (Oxford University Press, 1967)

It contains a lengthy Scripture index that allows you to locate quickly any data from ancient sources that may relate to your passage or book.

Helpful for its more than 800 individual articles on archaeological topics is:

E. M. Blaiklock and R. K. Harrison (eds.), *The New International Dictionary of Biblical Archaeology* (Zondervan Publishing House, 1983)

See also:

Robert F. Heizer, et al., *Archaeology: A Bibliographical Guide to the Basic Literature* (Garland Publishing, 1980)

A large number of individual articles on key subjects and findings related to the OT were gathered together in:

Edward F. Campbell, Jr., David Noel Freedman, and G. Ernest Wright (eds.), *The Biblical Archaeologist Reader*, 3 vols. (Doubleday, 1961– 1970)

3.6. Geographies and atlases

The newest geography of the Bible is one of the best:

Leslie J. Hoppe, *A Guide to the Lands of the Bible* (Michael Glazier, 1999)

Two older, yet still authoritative studies on Holy Land geography (weather, agriculture, topography, etc.) may be used with much profit:

Denis Baly, *The Geography of the Bible*, rev. ed. (Harper & Row, 1974)
Yohanan Aharoni, *The Land of the Bible: A Historical Geography*, rev. ed. (Westminster Press, 1980)

The best atlas for OT studies is also the easiest to use, and the most helpful in exegetical tasks. It is chock-full of maps, charts, and other illustrations, accompanied by clear explanatory notes. The many biblical passages to which the atlas is relevant are contained in a separate index, as well as with each illustration:

Yohanan Aharoni and Michael Avi-Yonah (eds.), *The Macmillan Bible Atlas* (Macmillan Co., 1968; rev. ed., 1977; 3d ed., 1993)

Others are also useful and accurate, including notably:

J. J. Bimson, et al. (eds.), *The New Bible Atlas,* repr. (Intervarsity Press, 1996)

Thomas C. Brisco and Thomas V. Brisco (eds.), *The Holman Bible Atlas: A Complete Guide to the Expansive Geography of Biblical History* (Broadman and Holman, 1998)

Carl G. Rasmussen (ed.), *The Zondervan NIV Atlas of the Bible* (Zondervan Publishing House, 1989)

Herbert G. May, et al. (eds.), *Oxford Bible Atlas*, 2d ed. (Oxford University Press, 1974)

Barry Beitzel (ed.), *The Moody Atlas of the Bible* (Moody Press, 1985)

3.7. *Historical criticism*

As it is most narrowly defined, historical criticism is concerned with the historical settings of biblical texts, including the establishing of names, dates, and times for events mentioned or attended to in a given passage. The aim of this sort of historical criticism is to arrive at a useful understanding of the relevant historical factors, in a form that elucidates them fully. Thus the historian goes well beyond the limits of the passage itself in establishing the historical factors and trends, more or less independently of the way they happen to be presented in the Bible.

However, historical criticism is a term also used to mean what is otherwise called the historical-critical method. This method has as its basic assumption the idea that "objective" biblical-historical study must treat the Bible like any other book, putting aside such "subjective" ideas as inspiration, authority, and divine causation. For obvious reasons, the historical-critical method is a subject of great debate as to its own "objectivity."

A lucid introduction to the special issues involved and the methodological assumptions is:

Edgar Krentz, *The Historical-Critical Method*, Guides to Biblical Scholarship (Fortress Press, 1975)

A properly motivated but inadequately documented attack on the historical-critical method may be found in:

Gerhard Maier, *The End of the Historical-Critical Method* (Concordia Publishing House, 1977)

Very helpful as a corrective to the kind of unchecked skepticism that has characterized some OT historical studies in the name of objectivity is:

Kenneth A. Kitchen, *Ancient Orient and Old Testament* (Intervarsity Fellowship, Tyndale Press, 1966)

For a perspective on the challenges and difficulties encountered in the historical study of the OT, sometimes with controversial conclusions about the evidence and what can be inferred from it, see these:

V. Phillips Long, *Israel's Past in Present Research: Essays on Ancient Israelite Historiography* (Eisenbrauns, 1999)

J. Maxwell Miller, *The Old Testament and the Historian*, Guides to Biblical Scholarship (Fortress Press, 1976)

John D. Levenson, *The Hebrew Bible, the Old Testament and Historical Criticism* (Westminster Press, 1993)

Niels Peter Lemche, *Prelude to Israel's Past: Background and Beginnings of Israelite History and Identity* (Hendrickson, 1998)

John Van Seters, *In Search of History: Historiography in the Ancient World and the Origins of Biblical History* (Eisenbrauns, 1997)

3.8. Tradition criticism

The study of the history of oral traditions as they functioned to preserve the literature and especially the history of ancient Israel before formalization in writing is called tradition criticism.

For a useful overview, read one of the following:

Douglas A. Knight, "Tradition History" in *The Anchor Bible Dictionary*, vol. 6, pp. 633–38 (Doubleday, 1992)

J. H. Hayes and C. R. Holladay, "Tradition Criticism," chap. 7 in *Biblical Exegesis: A Beginner's Handbook* (Westminster John Knox Press, 1997)

Some widely used introductions to this somewhat theoretical field are:

Jan Vansina, *Oral Tradition as History* (University of Wisconsin Press, 1990)

Douglas A. Knight, *Rediscovering the Traditions of Israel* (Scholars Press and the Society of Biblical Literature, 1973)

Walter Rast, *Tradition History and the Old Testament*, Guides to Biblical Scholarship (Fortress Press, 1972)

4. Literary Analysis

4.1. Parallel literature

The Bible is a unique book; there is nothing like it. There are, however, many individual literary works preserved from the ancient world that are remarkably similar to parts of the Bible. To ignore these valuable parallels where they exist is to impoverish an exegesis. Fortunately, the majority of the known parallels have been collected for easy reference.

The standard translation of (usually complete) texts parallel to the OT is found in the following large volume, which is recommended even though very expensive:

James B. Pritchard (ed.), *Ancient Near Eastern Texts Relating to the Old Testament*, 3d ed. with supplement (Princeton University Press, 1969)

Two abridgements are found in:

James B. Pritchard (ed.), *The Ancient Near East: An Anthology of Texts and Pictures* (Princeton University Press, 1958); Vol. 2: *The Ancient Near East: A New Anthology of Texts and Pictures* (Princeton University Press, 1976)

Both the full edition and the abridgements contain indexes of Scripture references for easy correlation to biblical passages. (The companion volumes for pictures are listed at 4.11.6.)

Much of the time, your interest will probably be focused toward parallel literature from the ancient Near East that is specifically religious in nature. Any of the following contain more comprehensive introductions and generally more helpful notes than Pritchard's volume, and all are virtually as complete with regard to important religious documents that parallel OT materials:

William W. Hallo and K. L. Younger (eds.), *The Context of Scripture* (Brill Academic Publishers, 1997)

Victor H. Matthews and Don C. Benjamin, *Old Testament Parallels: Laws and Stories from the Ancient Near East* (Paulist Press, 1997)

John H. Walton, *Ancient Israelite Literature in Its Cultural Context: A Survey of Parallels between Biblical and Ancient Near Eastern Texts* (Zondervan Publishing House, 1994)

Walter Beyerlin (ed.), *Near Eastern Religious Texts Relating to the Old Testament*, The Old Testament Library (Westminster Press, 1978)

For the important individual semantic parallels from the Late Bronze Age tablets found at Ugarit, there is a very useful collection built around words, terms, and concepts that occur in both Ugaritic and Hebrew. These include animals, plants, numerals, names, professions, social institutions, literary phrases, literary genres, etc.:

Loren Fisher (ed.), *Ras Shamra Parallels: The Texts from Ugarit and the Hebrew Bible*, 2 vols.; Analecta Orientalia 49, 50 (Pontifical Biblical Institute, 1972, 1976)

Each entry has a translation of the Ugaritic passage, textual notes, a bibliography, and an evaluation of the Ugaritic-Hebrew connections.

You can learn much about the beliefs of the Canaanites of Ugarit by reading for yourself their major myths. An excellent translation of these is by Coogan:

Michael Coogan, *Stories from Ancient Canaan* (Westminster Press, 1978)

Comparably valuable is:

Nicolas Wyatt, *Religious Texts from Ugarit* (Sheffield Academic Press, 1998)

4.2. Genre criticism

The criticism or analysis of genres (literary types) is usually limited to larger literary units and styles such as law, history, and wisdom. Often, however, individual scholars may use "genre" interchangeably with "form," so that there is no distinction between form criticism (see 4.5.1) and genre criticism, and thus no distinction between larger literary types (genres) and smaller, specific individual types (forms). Even though the distinction between the two types may be considered somewhat arbitrary, and even though it is a subjective decision as to whether a given literary type is general and large enough to be a genre or small and specific enough to be a form, the distinction is still useful and it is recommended that you follow it. Thus, for example, "narrative" is considered a whole genre, but a "census narrative" would be considered an individual form; "wisdom" is a whole genre, but a "numerical wisdom enumeration" would be considered a specific form; elegiac poetry might be frequent enough in the OT to be called a genre, whereas a "battle aftermath lament" such as 2 Samuel 1:19–27 would be specific enough to be considered a "form." As a rule, you should confine use of the term "genre" to literary types that are represented fairly widely by varying subtypes; the subtypes themselves are the forms.

The best, easiest-to-follow, overall introduction to genres (and forms as well) remains part 1 of Eissfeldt's *The Old Testament: An Introduction* (4.1.2).

A more detailed analysis, with examples, of the method of genre criticism is found in:

> D. Brent Sandy and Ronald L. Giese (eds.), *Cracking Old Testament Codes: A Guide to Interpreting Literary Genres of the Old Testament* (Broadman and Holman, 1995)

4.3. Redaction criticism

Redaction criticism concerns itself with how the various units that comprise a section or book of the OT were put together in their intermediate or final form. It therefore requires analysis of the work of the (anonymous) editors of the section or book, and is accordingly a very speculative kind of criticism since nothing is directly known about editorial activity or the editors themselves.

A useful introduction to the subject was written by Perrin, which, however, concentrates largely on the NT rather than the OT:

> Norman Perrin, *What Is Redaction Criticism?* Guides to Biblical Scholarship (Fortress Press, 1969)

For OT materials, a brief introduction to the method is found in:

J. H. Hayes and C. R. Holladay, "Redaction Criticism," chap. 8 in *Biblical Exegesis: A Beginner's Handbook* (Westminster John Knox Press, 1997)

An example of redaction criticism undertaken with a view to the application of its results to biblical theology is:

Simon J. DeVries, *From Old Revelation to New: A Tradition-Historical and Redaction-Critical Study of Temporal Transitions in Prophetic Prediction* (Wm. B. Eerdmans, 1994)

4.4. Literary criticism

The term "literary criticism" is used in several ways. For many years, literary criticism meant little more than source criticism (see 4.4.5). Occasionally it meant roughly what the term "historical criticism" is now used to describe (see 4.3.7). Increasingly, however, the term is used in its most basic meaning to refer to the process of analyzing and understanding parts of the Bible as literature, examining technique, style, and other features in order to gain an appreciation for the intention and results of a given portion as a literary composition.

For a brief overview of this type of criticism, you can read:

J. H. Hayes and C. R. Holladay, "Literary Criticism," chap. 5 in *Biblical Exegesis: A Beginner's Handbook* (Westminster John Knox Press, 1997)

A longer introduction, with somewhat controversial examples of the method applied, is:

David Robertson, *The Old Testament and the Literary Critic*, Guides to Biblical Scholarship (Fortress Press, 1977)

For more extensive examples of and arguments for the method, with an emphasis on source criticism within the definition of literary criticism, see:

Norman C. Habel and J. Coert Rylaarsdam (eds.), *Literary Criticism of the Old Testament* (Augsburg Fortress Press, 1994)
J. Cheryl Exum and David J. A. Clines, *The New Literary Criticism and the Hebrew Bible* (Trinity Press International, 1994)

Two of the best books on the topic, with special attention to the kinds of results useful to pastors and teachers in doing exegesis, are:

> Paul R. House (ed.), *Beyond Form Criticism: Essays in Old Testament Literary Criticism* (Eisenbrauns, 1992)
> Leland Ryken (ed.), *The Complete Literary Guide to the Bible* (Zondervan Publishing House, 1993)

4.5. Source criticism

Applicable mostly in the case of the Pentateuch, and to a lesser extent the historical books, source criticism attempted to discern the various written documents which the final editor (of the Pentateuch, for example) drew from in producing the finished work. This criticism is now often considered outdated since the human "sources" of the OT are far more complex and more difficult to recover or isolate than a few written documents would be. Even so, the general features of the documentary hypothesis of Graf and Wellhausen, which posits four main sources for the Pentateuch (J, E, D, P) and suggests approximate dates for each, are still accepted by many OT scholars. An introduction to source criticism (under its alternate appellation, literary criticism) is found in:

> Norman C. Habel, *Literary Criticism of the Old Testament*, Guides to Biblical Scholarship (Fortress Press, 1971)

4.6. Dating

For many years, the tendency among OT scholars was to date portions of Scripture on the basis of theories about the evolution of Israelite religion rather than on any intrinsic, objective criteria. The law was therefore dated late because it supposedly evidenced "developed" features, whereas the more "primitive" stories about Yahweh's leadership of the exodus, for example, could be dated early. Such hypothetical constructions are now largely out of favor, but great diversity still exists concerning the dating of various OT books and sections thereof. Dating books on the basis of linguistic features has always been inherently more objective in intent, but has suffered from a lack of specific knowledge. For poetry, there are some tentative approaches that would appear to offer hope. If your passage is poetry, you may be able to suggest a date for it—even if the context gives no clue—by consulting:

David A. Robertson, *Linguistic Evidence in Dating Early Hebrew Poetry* (Scholars Press, 1973)

Robertson provides a preliminary typology for dating poetry according to mostly morphological features.

Also still helpful is chapter 1 of:

W. F. Albright, *Yahweh and the Gods of Canaan* (Doubleday, 1968)

In the case of some poetry, and virtually all prose, there is very little agreed-upon evidence that allows for specific dating on the basis of linguistic features. You must rely primarily on the claims of the text itself and nonlinguistic features. Orthographic (spelling) features in a few cases may be indicative of date. In most cases, however, the orthography of the Hebrew OT is of no help. This is because early and late texts alike are written in the orthography of the Persian period (540–333 B.C.), since the texts from early times were conjoined and copied widely during the Restoration. Thus a single orthography was applied through the entire OT in both Hebrew and Aramaic. Only the small portions that partially escape this leveling process (such as some of the earliest poems) can be dated by the orthographic evidence. For how it's done, see:

David Noel Freedman, Francis Andersen, and A. Dean Forbes (eds.), *Studies in Hebrew and Aramaic Orthography* (Eisenbrauns, 1992)

or the older but still valuable:

Frank Moore Cross, Jr., and David Noel Freedman, *Early Hebrew Orthography* (American Oriental Society, 1952)

5. Form

5.1. Form criticism

The concern of form criticism is the isolation and analysis of specific literary types contained in a passage. From such an analysis the exegete can often discern something about the way the passage has been composed, its themes, its central interests, or even the type of situation in which it may have been employed (depending on the form) in ancient Israel. All of these bits of information may theoretically be deduced even if the context of the passage itself does not contain them, because study of all the various manifestations of the specific form throughout the Bible (and other ancient literature where it exists) allows certain generalizations to be applied to each usage.

Form criticism has often come under attack as a method that yields too little "meaning" from passages, and one that neglects other valid critical techniques. Form criticism has also earned something of a bad name by being applied by some scholars in an all-encompassing manner, and with an overconfidence in the insights it can provide. For example, some form-critical enthusiasts have used the technique to arrive at (what they regard as) firm conclusions about the dating, authorship, genuineness, originality, contextual propriety, historical validity, etc., of biblical passages, which the method in reality simply cannot support. It is more widely understood now that ancient writers (including the prophets, in whose books form criticism is especially employed) often borrowed forms from the ancient world in a tentative manner and reworked them. Their own inspired creativity was everywhere evident, and they were hardly slaves to a set of rules to which the forms (and parts of forms) they used could always be conformed. Ancient biblical writers and speakers thus took what they wanted from the existing forms (the typical) and produced new combinations or constructions (the unique).

Two helpful sources for understanding form criticism are available. A good introduction to the method is that of Tucker, who treats it systematically according to the four elements of structure, genre, setting, and intention:

> Gene M. Tucker, *Form Criticism of the Old Testament*, Guides to Biblical Scholarship (Fortress Press, 1971)

This collection of six essays explains the history of, as well as current trends in, form criticism. For understanding the goals and presuppositions of form criticism, as well as how it applies in various OT passages, see:

John H. Hayes (ed.), *Old Testament Form Criticism* (Trinity University Press, 1974)

On the specific relationship of form criticism to history, with examples, see:

Martin J. Buss, *Biblical Form Criticism in Its Context.* JSOT 274 (Sheffield Academic Press, 1999)

A classic, originally German-language introduction to OT form criticism, with examples of the method applied, is:

Klaus Koch, *The Growth of the Biblical Tradition: The Form-Critical Method* (Charles Scribner's Sons, 1969)

Best of all, a comprehensive series includes among its multiple volumes a discussion of all the individual literary forms in the OT, unit by unit. The volume in this series that covers your particular passage can profitably be consulted for specific advice—for a seasoned form critic's judgment on the pericope you are trying to exegete.

Rolf Knierim and Gene Tucker (eds.), *Forms of the Old Testament Literature* (Wm. B. Eerdmans, 1984–)

So far covered by *FOTL* are the following: Genesis; Exodus 1–18; 1–2 Kings; 1–2 Chronicles; Psalms 1–60; Job; Proverbs; Ruth; Song; Ecclesiastes; Esther; Isaiah 1–39; Ezekiel; Daniel; Minor Prophets Part 1; and Micah.

5.2. The relationship of form to structure

There is no way to discover a literary form or to identify it properly without first identifying the various items of which it is composed (its content) and the way that those items are arranged in relation to one another and in relation to the larger context (the structure). In other words, the exegete faces the danger of putting the cart before the horse if he or she jumps too quickly to the conclusion that a passage contains, or is composed in the manner of, form X, simply on the basis of some key words that form X usually contains, or some other stylistic features normally associated with form X. One can actually go so far as to ignore the majority of the evidence for form typology and mistakenly categorize a form. Alternatively, one can place so much emphasis on a strictly form-critical methodology that many exegetically significant features not contained in the results of the form-critical analysis are simply forgotten.

First, then, be sure that you understand the elements or "ingredients" of the passage's content and understand at least tentatively how the elements are structured before identifying a form. The proper identification of the form(s) may subsequently help you refine your identification of the elements and the structure, but don't let the known typical features of the form dominate the way you analyze the specific features of the passage. Rather, it is just the other way around: The specific features of the passage tell you how much or how little any forms that happen to be present influence the passage, if at all— and to what extent the form is pure, adapted, "broken," or incomplete.

6. Structure

6.1. Definitions

Five similar terms are used in OT studies with varying degrees of frequency and with at least two very different meanings. Three of these terms—structuralism, structural exegesis, and structural analysis—usually are employed to refer to a kind of linguistic analysis that is applied to biblical studies. Structuralism (the most common of these terms) is concerned largely with certain special, rather technically defined relationships between or within the words in a sentence. The structuralist seeks to understand the rules by which language functions, on the theory that those rules can lead to a deeper understanding of the structure (and meaning) of the components of sentences and of sentences themselves. The following books explain structuralism and provide some examples of its possible use in biblical sentences:

Roland Barthes, et al., *Structural Analysis and Biblical Exegesis: Interpretational Essays* (Pickwick Press, 1974)

Jean Calloud, *Structural Analysis of Narrative* (Fortress Press and Scholars Press, 1976)

Daniel Patte, *The Religious Dimensions of Biblical Texts: Greimas's Structural Semiotics and Biblical Exegesis* (Society of Biblical Literature, 1990)

Daniel Patte, *Structural Exegesis for New Testament Critics* (Trinity Press International, 1996)

Best for the beginner to learn from, however, is:

Daniel Patte, *What Is Structural Exegesis? Guides to Biblical Scholarship* (Fortress Press, 1976)

Two other terms—structural criticism and structural studies—are usually employed to describe the way that larger units of text (passages) are composed of their various elements of content. The latter two terms, in other words, refer generally to the content structure of a passage, whereas the former three terms refer mostly to concern for the linguistic patterns in individual sentences.

Structuralism (the specialized linguistic analysis) is technical and narrowly applied, and is also less interested in the historical, cultural, or theological, except in a secondary way. Thus it is not likely that you will find occasion to use it widely in any given exegesis. Like "linguistic analysis" in philosophy, the results are occasionally stellar, but too often meager. Nevertheless, the diligent student may find the task well worth the effort in particular passages.

For an understanding of the broader method of structural studies, how passages are put together from their constituent elements, how their structure may be deduced and outlined, and the significance for exegesis, there is a very fine, short book, filled with helpful examples:

Robert C. Culley, *Studies in the Structure of Hebrew Narrative* (Fortress Press and Scholars Press, 1976)

The broader method of structural studies is far more likely to be of constant value to exegetes, as is the broader discipline of rhetorical criticism whose methods may generally be considered to encompass structural studies as well.

6.2. Rhetorical criticism

Rhetorical criticism looks at how a literary unit (usually a passage) is put together. Whereas form criticism tends to emphasize the typical and general, rhetorical criticism concentrates on the genius of a passage—that which is personal, specific, unique, or original. The rhetorical critic seeks to understand the inspired writer's logic, style, and purpose. To do this, emphasis must be placed on (a) the patterns found within the literary unit; (b) the individual stylistic devices that contribute to the overall impact of the whole unit; and (c) the relationship of the parts to the whole. Rhetorical criticism is most often synchronic (concerned with the passage as it stands now) rather than diachronic (concerned with the theoretical history of how the passage might have been transmitted, mutated, reshaped, or edited before reaching its present form).

As usually practiced, rhetorical criticism emphasizes the structure of the canonical text, yet uses the most modern, reliable techniques to implement this emphasis. For the original statement of the need to go beyond the limits of form criticism to rhetorical criticism, see:

> James Muilenburg, "Form Criticism and Beyond" (*Journal of Biblical Literature* 88 [1969], 1–18)

For a more comprehensive analysis, with examples and bibliographical helps, see any or all of the following:

> Roland Meynet, *Rhetorical Analysis: An Introduction to Biblical Rhetoric* (Sheffield Academic Press, 1999)
> L. J. De Regt, J. P. Fokkelman, and J. De Waard (eds.), *Literary Structure and Rhetorical Strategies in the Hebrew Bible* (Eisenbrauns, 1996)
> Duane F. Watson and Alan J. Hauser, *Rhetorical Criticism of the Bible: A Comprehensive Bibliography with Notes on History and Method* (E. J. Brill, 1994)
> Dale Patrick and Allen Scult, *Rhetoric and Biblical Interpretation*, JSOT 82 (Almond Press, 1990)

Examples of rhetorical criticism applied to various biblical passages are found in:

> James W. Watts, *Reading Law: The Rhetorical Shaping of the Pentateuch* (Sheffield Academic Press, 1999)
> Phyllis Trible, *Rhetorical Criticism: Context, Method, and the Book of Jonah* (Augsburg Fortress Press, 1994)
> Pieter Van Der Lugt, *Rhetorical Criticism and the Poetry of the Book of Job* (E. J. Brill, 1995)
> Jared J. Jackson and Martin Kessler (eds.), *Rhetorical Criticism: Essays in Honor of James Muilenburg* (Pickwick Press, 1974)

Part of analyzing a passage's rhetoric involves identifying its figures of speech. For this task, consult the classic:

E. W. Bullinger, *Figures of Speech Used in the Bible*, repr. (Baker Book House, 1968)

6.3. Formula criticism

Certain groups of words (sometimes individual words) tend to appear in different passages in similar ways. When a word group functions consistently to express a given essential idea, yet in a variety of contexts, it is called a formula. Poetry seems to have many more formulae than does prose. Some examples (in translation) of common, well-known formulae are: "Thus says the Lord," "says the Lord of Hosts," "How long will you ...?" "In that day," "In the latter days," "Great is the Lord and greatly to be praised." Such formulae appear in a variety of passages. Understanding how formulae function, how they represent "building blocks" within literary units, how they relate to the meter of a passage, etc., is the goal of formula criticism. Because formula criticism emphasizes the comparison of formula contexts, it is especially relevant to biblical context (step 9) and to structure (step 6). Two books explain the process and its implications for exegesis:

Robert C. Culley, *Oral Formulaic Language in the Biblical Psalms* (University of Toronto Press, 1967)
William R. Watters, *Formula Criticism and the Poetry of the Old Testament* (Walter de Gruyter, 1976)

6.4. Poetry analysis (poetics)

Poetics is a vast study. Nevertheless, a proper feel for the poetry of the OT is not so hard to come by that it should be avoided. In fact, with a reasonable investment of time the student of the OT can move rather quickly from relative ignorance to relative competence in analyzing poetry. It is especially important to be able to recognize the types of parallelism and the metrical structure that characterize a given passage of poetry, and good sources are available for each.

For a brief but clear introduction to both issues, see:

Norman K. Gottwald, "Poetry, Hebrew" in *The Interpreter's Dictionary of the Bible* (Abingdon Press, 1972), vol. 3, pp. 829–38

For a more comprehensive coverage, see:

Frank Moore Cross and David Noel Freedman, *Studies in Ancient Yahwistic Poetry* (Wm. B. Eerdmans, 1997)

David L. Peterson and Kent H. Richards, *Interpreting Hebrew Poetry* (Augsburg Fortress Press, 1994)

James L. Kugel, *The Idea of Biblical Poetry: Parallelism and Its History*, repr. (Johns Hopkins University Press, 1998)

and the old but still useful classic:

George Buchanan Gray, *The Forms of Hebrew Poetry, with Prolegomenon by David Noel Freedman* (KTAV Publishing House, 1970)

To analyze certain types of poetic parallelism effectively, you will need to learn how "fixed pairs" of words function in OT poems. The best (and clearest) introduction to this analysis, with hundreds of easy-to-follow examples, is:

Stanley Gevirtz, *Patterns in the Early Poetry of Israel* (University of Chicago Press, 1964)

On Hebrew meter, see:

Douglas K. Stuart, *Studies in Early Hebrew Meter* (Scholars Press and Harvard Semitic Museum, 1976)

The situation as regards meter is more difficult for the student, since conflicting theories of metrical composition still persist. Nevertheless, whichever of the four most common approaches ("stress" meter, semantic parallelism meter, alternating meter, syllabic meter) is used, if used consistently it will provide the student with an objective means of discerning and evaluating the relative length of lines of poetry and also the way that lines may be grouped together into couplets and triplets (often called bicola and tricola), or large units (sometimes called strophes).

Two important books on Hebrew meter are sufficiently technical and complex in their analyses that only the more advanced Hebrew student could make routine use of them. The best is:

Stephen Geller, *Parallelism in Early Biblical Poetry*, Harvard Semitic Monographs 20 (Scholars Press, 1979)

Intriguing and somewhat controversial are:

Michael O'Connor, *Hebrew Verse Structure* (Eisenbrauns, 1980)
Donald R. Vance, *The Question of Meter in Biblical Hebrew Poetry* (Edwin Mellen Press, 2001)

7. Grammar

7.1. Reference grammars

Properly used, reference grammars are a ready source of exegetically relevant information. The grammars often collect together many or all of the instances of a certain type of grammatical phenomenon. When you refer to the grammar for information on such a phenomenon, you are thus provided with a list of parallels and an explanation of how the phenomenon functions in the OT. That can be just the sort of information you need to help you make certain exegetical decisions.

If you need to refresh your knowledge of Hebrew using a basic grammar, the following four are excellent:

Gary D. Pratico and Miles Van Pelt, *Basics of Biblical Hebrew* (Zondervan Publishing House, 2001)
Duane Garrett, *Reading Biblical Hebrew* (Broadman and Holman, 2001)
Choon L. Seow, *A Grammar for Biblical Hebrew* (Abingdon Press, 1995)
Thomas O. Lambdin, *Introduction to Biblical Hebrew* (Charles Scribner's Sons, 1971)

For Hebrew the classic reference grammar has been:

F. W. Gesenius, *Hebrew Grammar*, rev. by E. Kautzsch, 2d English ed., ed. and tr. by A. E. Cowley (Clarendon Press, 1910)

Three newer grammars offer a fine array of sophisticated insight into the grammatical structures and nuances of Hebrew. Don't be misled by the title of the first one (*An Outline*); it's an erudite overview of all significant syntactical features, and thus faster to use than the other two, which are, as well, remarkably erudite.

Ronald J. Williams, *Hebrew Syntax: An Outline* (University of Toronto Press, 1976)

Paul Joüon, *A Grammar of Biblical Hebrew*, 2 vols. (Pontifical Biblical Institute, 1996)

Bruce K. Waltke and M. O'Connor, *An Introduction to Biblical Hebrew Syntax* (Eisenbrauns, 1990)

Helpful both for its collection of instances of special grammatical features from throughout the Hebrew Bible, and for its solutions for many problematic grammatical issues, is:

Alexander Sperber, *A Historical Grammar of Biblical Hebrew* (E. J. Brill, 1966)

For Aramaic grammatical features, you will probably find almost everything you need in one of these:

Frederick E. Greenspahn, *An Introduction to Aramaic* (SBL Scholars Press, 1999)

Alger F. Johns, *A Short Grammar of Biblical Aramaic* (Andrews University Press, 1982)

Franz Rosenthal, *A Grammar of Biblical Aramaic* (Harrassowitz, 1961)

William B. Stevenson, *Grammar of Palestinian Jewish Aramaic* (Wipf and Stock Publishers, 2000)

If you wish to refer to data relevant to the Aramaic grammar from the entire Old Aramaic period (earliest texts through the end of the Persian empire in 333 B.C.), a technical, very comprehensive source is:

Stanislav Segert, *Altaramäische Grammatik* (Verlag Enzyklopadie, VEB, 1975)

A coverage of Targumic Aramaic is found in:

Marcus David, *A Manual of Babylonian Jewish Aramaic* (University Press of America, 1981)

Vitzchok Frank, *Grammar for Gemara: An Introduction to Babylonian Aramaic*, 2d. rev. ed. (Philipp Feldheim, 1994)

Two useful grammars for the Septuagint are available, though the first tends to concentrate on morphology:

Henry St. J. Thackeray, *A Grammar of the Old Testament in Greek according to the Septuagint* (Cambridge University Press, 1909)
F. C. Conybeare and St. George Stock, *Grammar of Septuagint Greek:
With Selected Readings, Vocabularies, and Updated Indexes* (Hendrickson, 1995)

If you do exegesis of passages of poetry, especially the Psalms
or Job, you may find in the secondary literature frequent reference
to two languages, Ugaritic and Phoenician, which are very similar
to Hebrew. Even if you have not studied these languages formally,
you may be able to understand something of their relevance
and helpfulness on specific points by consulting the following
grammars:

Stanislav Segert, *Basic Grammar of the Ugaritic Language: With Selected
Texts and Glossary* (University of California Press, 1985)
Daniel Sivan, *A Grammar of the Ugaritic Language* (Brill Academic Pub-
lishers, 1997)
Cyrus H. Gordon, *Ugaritic Textbook*, rev. repr. (Pontifical Biblical Insti-
tute, 1998)
Zellig S. Harris, *A Grammar of the Phoenician Language* (American Ori-
ental Society, 1936)
Stanislav Segert, *A Grammar of Phoenician and Punic* (C. H. Beck, 1976)

For Syriac, a language necessary for competence in OT textual criticism, three recent grammars may be commended:

Wheeler M. Thackston, *Introduction to Syriac: An Elementary Grammar
with Readings from Syriac Literature* (IBEX Publishers, 2000)
Takamitsu Muroaka, *Classical Syriac: A Basic Grammar* (Harrassowitz,
1997)
Michael P. Weitzman, *The Syriac Version of the Old Testament: An Introduction* (Cambridge University Press, 1999)

For Akkadian, the language of hundreds of thousands of documents from Babylon and Assyria, many of which directly bear on biblical knowledge, consider:

John Huehnergard and Jo Ann Hackett (eds.), *A Grammar of Akkadian*
(Scholars Press, 1997)

7.2. Other technical sources

It is sometimes helpful to be able to refer to a comparative grammar, one that considers Hebrew forms and features in the context of those of other Semitic languages. The following are all useful in this regard:

Patrick R. Bennett, *Comparative Semitic Linguistics: A Manual* (Eisenbrauns, 1998)

E. Lapinski, *Semitic Languages: Outline of a Comparative Grammar*, OLA 80 (Peeters, 1997)

Gideon Goldenberg, *Studies in Semitic Linguistics: Selected Writings* (Magnes Press, 1998)

To understand Hebrew in the more immediate context of the Canaanite language family, see both of the following:

Zellig S. Harris, *Development of the Canaanite Dialects* (American Oriental Society, 1939)

William L. Moran, "The Hebrew Language in Its Northwest Semitic Background," in G. Ernest Wright (ed.), *The Bible and the Ancient Near East* (Doubleday, 1961)

Orthography (spelling analysis) is a technical study within the field of grammar that can occasionally help the exegete unravel aspects of a difficult text. The classic study compares Hebrew with Phoenician, Aramaic, and Moabite during the OT period, based on the evidence of the inscriptions dating to OT times:

Frank Moore Cross, Jr., and David Noel Freedman, *Early Hebrew Orthography* (American Oriental Society, 1952)

This has been helpfully updated in various aspects by:

David Noel Freedman, Francis Andersen, and A. Dean Forbes (eds.), *Studies in Hebrew and Aramaic Orthography* (Eisenbrauns, 1992)

8. Lexical Analysis

8.1. Lexicons

A lexicon is a dictionary. The fact that the term "lexicon" has been used instead of the term "dictionary" by biblical and classical scholars is simply a quirk of linguistic history, well deserving of a word study of its own.

The lexicons are valuable sources of information about the words they list. Lexicons often devote lengthy articles (mini "word studies" or, better, concept studies) to those words that are especially interesting or significant theologically, and also to words that have any unusual or crucial features. It is a mistake to launch upon a word study or even to comment at length about the usage of a word in Scripture without first consulting the relevant lexicons.

The Hebrew lexicon to use (if possible) is:

Ludwig Koehler and Walther Baumgartner [rev. by Walther Baumgartner and Johann J. Stamm], *Hebrew and Aramaic Lexicon of the Old Testament*, 5 vols. (Brill Academic Publishers, 1994–2000)

This lexicon is the world's standard. It is a massive and expensive work, and therefore it is also wise to consider a fine abridgment, one that preserves virtually all the essential information of its comprehensive "parent":

William L. Holladay, *A Concise Hebrew and Aramaic Lexicon of the Old Testament* (Wm. B. Eerdmans, 1972)

Currently under way and nearing completion is a most welcome, massive lexicon project:

David J. A. Clines (ed.), *The Dictionary of Classical Hebrew*, 5 vols. (Sheffield Academic Press, vols. 1–4, 1994–2001)

Much less reliable, though still widely used (mainly because its copyright protection is gone and therefore it is cheaply available and sometimes bundled with or linked to various computer concordances), is:

Francis Brown, S. R. Driver, and Charles A. Briggs, *A Hebrew and English Lexicon of the Old Testament* (Clarendon Press, 1907; repr. 1962, 1966)

BDB is still somewhat useful because of the sheer volume of its fine articles, but it is somewhat outdated because it lacks cognate information from Ugaritic and other recent finds. Moreover, many of its suggested etymologies (histories of word origins and their relation to Semitic word roots) are often unacceptable.

For biblical Aramaic, the standard Hebrew lexicons all have an Aramaic section.

For Aramaic outside the Bible, especially in the Targums, a traditional source in English has been:

> Marcus Jastrow, *A Dictionary of the Targumim, the Talmud Babli and Yerushalmi, and the Midrashic Literature*, 2 vols., 2d ed. (1962; repr. Pardes Publishing House, 1950)

If you can read Latin, an excellent Aramaic lexicon is yours to use:

> Ernesto Vogt, *Lexicon Linguae Aramaicae Veteris Testamenti Documentis Antiquis Illustratum* (Pontifical Biblical Institute, 1971)

For the Septuagint, nothing excels:

> J. Eynikel, E. Hauspie, J. Lust, and A. Rahlfs (eds.), *Greek-English Lexicon of the Septuagint*, 2 vols. (American Bible Society, 1993, 1998)

Still useful is:

> W. Bauer, F. W. Gingrich, and F. W. Danker, *A Greek-English Lexicon of the New Testament and Other Early Christian Literature*, 2d ed. (University of Chicago Press, 1979)

Also often useful, but plagued by occasionally misleading Septuagint definitions, is:

> Henry O. Liddell and Robert Scott, *A Greek-English Lexicon*, rev. by Henry Stuart Jones and Roderick McKenzie; 9th ed. (Clarendon Press, 1940)

See also:

> E. A. Barber, et al. (eds.), *Supplement to A Greek-English Lexicon* (Oxford University Press, 1968)

For working from the Syriac Peshitta, use:

> R. Payne Smith, *A Compendious Syriac Dictionary*, ed. by J. Payne Smith (Clarendon Press, 1903; repr. 1957)

The massive *Latin Dictionary* of Lewis and Short is excellent for the Vulgate and other Latin texts:

Charlton T. Lewis and Charles Short, *A Latin Dictionary* [also titled *A New Latin Dictionary*; first published as *Harper's Latin Dictionary*] (New York, 1879; repr. Oxford University Press, 1979)

Since much lexical information about OT Hebrew has come from Assyrian/Babylonian and Ugaritic sources, from time to time you may find it necessary to consult the lexicons for these languages.

For Assyrian/Babylonian, use wherever possible the multivolume *CAD*:

Ignace Gelb, Benno Landsberger, A. Leo Oppenheim, Erika Reiner, et al. (eds.), *The Chicago Assyrian Dictionary* (Oriental Institute of the University of Chicago, 1956–)

For those who can read German, von Soden's dictionary is still useful:

Wolfram von Soden, *Akkadisches Handwörterbuch* (Harrassowitz, 1965)

An affordable paperback is:

Jeremy Black, et al. (eds.), *A Concise Dictionary of Akkadian* (Harrassowitz Verlag, 2000)

For Ugaritic words, the comprehensive lexicon is in German:

Joseph Aisleitner, *Wörterbuch der ugaritischen Sprache*, 4th ed. (Akademie-Verlag, 1974)

However, the third part of Gordon's *Ugaritic Textbook* (7.1) is a rather extensive glossary with English equivalents.

A Phoenician-Punic lexicon is also available:

Richard Tomback, *A Comparative Semitic Lexicon of the Phoenician and Punic Languages* (Scholars Press, 1978)

8.2. Concordances

A concordance lists the places where a given word occurs throughout the Bible (or some other literary collection). Concordances can help you determine the usage, distribution, and contextualizations of any given word (see 8.3) and are thus valuable tools for lexical analysis. It is almost impossible to do word (concept) studies without concordances, and almost impossible to do thorough exegesis without word (concept) studies.

Computer concordances are much faster and much more powerful than book concordances. Any of the various computer concordances can give information quickly, many allow original-language searches, and some are available for free via various Web sites. Two stand out for their true exegetical sophistication (the rich number of ways that Hebrew, Greek, and Aramaic grammatical and lexical information can be ascertained, and/or combined and/or assembled for exegetical use).

The very best is:

AcCordance (Macintosh), also called Gramcord (PC), available from the Gramcord Institute [www.gramcord.org] (360-576-3000; 2218 NE Brookview Dr., Vancouver, WA 98686, U.S.A. E-mail: schol ars@GRAMCORD.org)

Comparable, though somewhat less sophisticated in its grammatical search capabilities, is:

BibleWorks (Windows), available from Hermeneutika [bibleworks.com] (406-837-2244; (800) 74-BIBLE; Hermeneutika, P.O. Box 2200, Bigfork, MT 59911-2200, U.S.A. E-mail: sales@bibleworks.com)

Book concordances remain popular. Their strength can be the fact that they are the result of judicious choices made by scholars who have chosen what to include and what to exclude, so that even though they are far less comprehensive than and not nearly as versatile as the computer concordances, they provide at a glance some of the key sorts of information most exegetes are looking for. Any of the following may prove useful to you:

John R. Kohlenberger, III, and James A. Swanson, *The Hebrew-English Concordance to the Old Testament* (Zondervan Publishing House, 1998)

Abraham S. Evans (ed.), *A New Concordance of the Old Testament Using the Hebrew and Aramaic Text* (Baker Book House, 1989)

Robert L. Thomas (ed.), *New American Standard Exhaustive Concordance of the Bible with Hebrew-Aramaic and Greek Dictionaries* (Broadman and Holman, 1990)

Eliezer Katz, *Topical Concordance of the Old Testament Using the Hebrew and Aramaic Text* (Baker Book House, 1992)

An older standard and still useful book concordance for the Hebrew OT is Mandelkern's. It is written in Latin and Hebrew only, and lists words in a somewhat complicated order (partly by context within a given book rather than by successive references), but these drawbacks are minor:

Solomon Mandelkern, *Veteris Testamenti Concordantiae Hebraicae atque Chaldaicae*, 8th ed. (P. Shalom Publications, 1988)

Mandelkern's concordance is becoming difficult to find, however. Fortunately, a new, comparably massive Hebrew book concordance has appeared. It is harder to use at first, being written entirely in Hebrew (including the chapter numbers for various books), but it has an innovative format and several valuable features, such as word-frequency counts, fully vocalized context citations, and the inclusion of common phrases rather than merely individual words. It also contains a very helpful introduction explaining clearly how to use the concordance:

Abraham Even-Shoshan (ed.), *A New Concordance of the Old Testament*, 2d ed., introduction by John H. Sailhamer (Kiryat-Sefer Publishing House and Baker Book House, 1997)

A somewhat easier-to-use, though less complete, concordance is:

Gerhard Lisowsky, *Konkordanz zum hebräischen Alten Testament* (Württembergische Bibelanstalt, 1958)

For King James-Hebrew connections the standard concordance is:

George V. Wigram, *The Englishman's Hebrew and Chaldee Concordance of the Old Testament* (Samuel Bagster & Sons, 3d ed. 1874; repr. Zondervan Publishing House, 1978)

For the Septuagint, a complete book concordance exists. In analyzing the text of a passage, you must analyze the Septuagint wording. The only way to know whether the Septuagint wordings are unique, unusual, or common is to consult the concordance, which gives the Hebrew word equivalents for the Greek word chosen by the Septuagint translators.

> Edwin Hatch and Henry A. Redpath, *A Concordance to the Septuagint and the Other Greek Versions of the Old Testament,* 3d ed., 2 vols. including R. A. Kraft and E. Tov, "Introductory Essay" and Takamitsu Muraoka, *Hebrew/Aramaic Index to the Septuagint: Keyed to the Hatch-Redpath Concordance* (Baker Book House, 1999)

A brief but very useful (and inexpensive) one-volume Septuagint concordance is also available:

> George Morrish, *A Concordance of the Septuagint* (Samuel Bagster & Sons; repr. Zondervan Publishing House, 1976)

See also:

> Bernard Alwyn Taylor, *The Analytical Lexicon to the Septuagint: A Complete Parsing Guide* (Zondervan Publishing House, 1994)

There are also special concordances to Qumran texts, to parts of the Targum, to some individual OT books, to certain ancient writers, etc. Fitzmyer's *Bibliography* (see Introduction) contains ample bibliographical data on such special concordances for those not infrequent occasions when you will find it necessary to pursue in detail a word's usage substantially beyond the biblical evidence. For the books of the Apocrypha, there is a book concordance keyed to English words but listing the Greek equivalents:

> Lester T. Whitelocke (ed.), *An Analytical Concordance of the Books of the Apocrypha* (University Press of America, 1978)

An English-language equivalent, computer-generated, is found in:

> *A Concordance to the Apocrypha/Deuterocanonical Books of the Revised Standard Version* (Wm. B. Eerdmans, William Collins Sons & Co., 1983)

8.3. Word studies (concept studies)

A word (concept) study is a thorough analysis of the meaning(s) of a word or wording designed to arrive at its *specific* meaning in a given passage—what concept the word or wording connotes, and, as appropriate, what other words or wordings may connote the same essential concept. There are various ways to approach this sort of study, but the following outline will serve as a basic guide. In any case, a "word study" seeks to establish how the word or wording under investigation is used (1) in general, (2) in various contexts, and (3) in the passage itself. The steps to establish this are generally:

1. Using a concordance—computer or book—find where all the OT occurrences of the word or wording are. If the word or wording is common, think in terms of groups of occurrences; if it is rare, you may be able to examine all the usages in detail. Because of the magnitude of the enterprise, you may find it advisable to set more narrow limits (e.g., "the Meaning of זנה [prostitution/ prostitute] in Hosea").

2. Using other aids such as lexicons, take cognizance of the non-OT usages of the word or wording (in inscriptions, rabbinic literature, etc.).

3. Using lexicons, take note of any cognates in other languages you are able to work in. Try to identify also any synonyms of the word or wording, because a given concept can be connoted by different wordings, and it ultimately is the concept behind the word or wordings in your passage that you want to be sure you understand.

4. Examine the biblical usage, trying to establish the various ranges of meaning that the word or wording and its cognates seem to have. Bear in mind here also that a concept can be connoted by various words or wordings, and there may be a number of synonyms or closely related terms that will come to your attention and ultimately inform your judgment as you seek to connect your word or wording with its actual meaning (concept) in your passage. Part of the reason for this is that what we call "definition" is established not merely by trying to say what a word means, but also by being sure to try to say what it doesn't mean. (Example: Is the word "man" to be understood in a given context as *man* as opposed to *woman* or *man* as opposed to *child* or *man* as opposed to *animal* or *man* as opposed to *supernatural being* or *man* as opposed to *coward*, etc.?)

5. Examine the distribution of the word or wording. Much can be learned about the meaning this way. Is the word or wording used only or mostly by the prophets, for example? That might

tell you a great deal about its meaning. Is it used only or mostly in legal formulas? In certain kinds of expressions? Look for patterns wherever possible.

6.   Establish the key usages—those which are unambiguous enough that they really pin down the meaning (concept) in a definite way.

7.   Center on the function of the word or wording in the passage itself. Bring all you have learned in the study so far to bear on the passage, relating the specific use and meaning in the passage to the ranges of use and meaning known from elsewhere.

8.   Offer a paraphrase, synonyms, a summary statement, or all of these to your reader or congregation as a means of defining the word or wording. That is, give your own "dictionary" definition of the word, not just in its general use or uses, but according to its use in the passage itself. Again, remember that the concept is the ultimate goal and the word or wording functions not in itself alone but always in the role of pointing to a concept.

On the theory behind word studies see:

Moisés Silva, *Biblical Words and Their Meaning: An Introduction to Lexical Semantics* (Zondervan Publishing House, 1983)

8.4. Theological dictionaries

The theological dictionaries provide the reader with the results of careful word/concept studies. Obviously they must limit themselves to the broad, general usage of words and cannot usually focus on individual passages. But they are nevertheless invaluable as time-saving, informative exegetical resources. It is important not to accept blindly the conclusions of any theological dictionary article, however. A given writer's view can be slanted. It is best to follow with a critical eye the arguments and the evidence contained in the article.

The *TDOT* theological dictionary is thorough, erudite, and invaluable as a reference tool:

G. Johannes Botterweck and Helmer Ringgren (eds.), *Theological Dictionary of the Old Testament*, vols. 1–10, through '*zb* (Wm. B. Eerdmans, 1974–1999). In progress; full set not yet complete.

Extensive coverage of words and themes is also found in:

Willem A. VanGemeren (gen. ed.), *New International Dictionary of Old Testament Theology and Exegesis* (Zondervan Publishing House, 1998), 5 vols., also on CD-ROM (2001)

and in:

Ernst Jenni and Claus Westerman (eds.), *Theological Lexicon of the Old Testament*, 3 vols., repr. (Hendrickson, 1997)

A very useful two-volume theological dictionary should remain for some years to come a fine source for careful analysis of Hebrew words. Its articles are briefer than the corresponding articles in *TDOT* but by the same token are often more readable:

R. Laird Harris, Gleason Archer, and Bruce K. Waltke (eds.), *Theological Wordbook of the Old Testament*, 2 vols. (Moody Press, 1980)

There is still much to be learned from:

Johannes B. Bauer (ed.), *Encyclopedia of Biblical Theology*, 3 vols. (Sheed & Ward, 1970)

The older *TDNT* provides useful background information on OT terms with equivalents in the NT:

Gerhard Kittel and Gerhard Friedrich (eds.), *Theological Dictionary of the New Testament*, 10 vols., including index vol. (Wm. B. Eerdmans, 1964–1976)

Note: You can also use with great profit the major Bible dictionaries, which contain detailed articles on hundreds of key words and concepts. That is, the best article on "faith" might easily be found in, say, the *International Standard Bible Encyclopedia* or the *Anchor Bible Dictionary*, rather than in *any* of the theological dictionaries!

8.5. Inscriptions

Reading and analyzing inscriptions is a specialty that requires linguistic and philological training beyond the interests of most students and pastors. Nevertheless, a detailed word (concept) study may well take you to the inscriptional evidence. There are many fine analytical collections of inscriptions, in various languages, with varying contents. While many of the important inscriptions are translated in Pritchard's *ANET* (see 4.4.1), their vocabulary is not analyzed there. The following works contain in their titles clear descriptions of their respective contents:

Jacob Hoftijzer, et al., *Dictionary of the North-West Semitic Inscriptions*, 2 vols. (E. J. Brill, 1995)

Markus Bockmuehl, et al., *Ancient Hebrew Inscriptions: Corpus and Concordance* (Cambridge University Press, 1991)

John C. L. Gibson, *Textbook of Syrian Semitic Inscriptions: Vol. I, Hebrew and Moabite Inscriptions; Vol. II, Aramaic Inscriptions* (Oxford University Press, 1971, 1975)

Walter Aufrecht and John C. Hurd, *A Synoptic Concordance of Aramaic Inscriptions* (Biblical Research Associates, Scholars Press, 1975)

A still useful source is in German:

M. Donner and W. Rollig, *Kanaanäische und aramäische Inschriften*, 2d ed. (Harrassowitz, 1966)

9. Biblical Context

9.1. Chain reference lists

Many Bible editions in English contain what is colloquially called a "chain" reference list. In a separate column, or at the end of each verse, reference is given to passages elsewhere in the Bible which are in some way similar to or connected with that verse. None of these reference lists is entirely reliable or consistent, and many suggest references that are farfetched or unreasonable. Nevertheless, these lists can often lead you quickly to parallel or related passages containing similar concepts but not necessarily containing the same words found in the passage you are working on, and thus not to be found by the use of a concordance. Several Bible editions contain especially ample reference lists, including:

The Thompson Chain Reference Bible (Kirkbride Bible Co., 1998)—KJV
Harper Study Bible (HarperCollins, 1991)—NRSV

New American Standard Bible, Reference Edition (Broadman and Holman, 1999)—NASB

9.2. Topical concordances

Most students are familiar with word concordances (see 4.8.2). A word concordance can serve both to facilitate "word studies" and to guide the student to biblical context data. For the latter purpose, the concordance is used as a quick means of searching the OT (and NT) for: (1) parallel passages containing the word; and (2) parallel passages containing related topics or concepts that are found by reference to their characteristic vocabulary.

In addition to word concordances, however, there are topical concordances, which group together biblical passages related to one another by a common topic or theme (concept). They can be immensely valuable in suggesting to you other passages related to the one you are working on. In a sense, the topical concordances do what the reference lists do, only in much more detail and usually with the entire text of related passages printed out for immediate analysis.

For a convenient grouping of the complete text of Scripture passages relating to given doctrines (arranged by the classical categories, i.e., God, Christ, salvation, etc.), see:

Walter A. Elwell, *Topical Analysis of the Bible* (Baker Book House, 1991)
John J. Davis, *Handbook of Basic Bible Texts* (Zondervan Publishing House, 1984)

The following are also useful:

Orville J. Nave, *Nave's Topical Bible* (Moody Press, 1974)
Charles R. Joy, *Harper's Topical Concordance*, rev. and enl. ed. (Harper & Row, 1976)
Edward Viening (ed.), *The Zondervan Topical Bible* (Zondervan Publishing House, 1969)
Steve Bond (ed.), *Holman Concise Topical Concordance* (Holman Bible Publishers, 1999)

9.3. Commentaries and biblical context

One of the tasks of a commentator is to bring to the attention of the reader the manner in which a passage relates to the book in which it is found, and to the wider biblical context as well. The insights of a commentator usually go beyond what you can happen upon by using references and concordances. Therefore, it pays to consult several exegetically oriented commentaries, both classical and modern, looking specifically for indications of intrabiblical relationships. For specific bibliographical information on exegetical commentary series, see 4.11.6.

9.4. Apocrypha and Pseudepigrapha

Ancient Judaism produced certain religious works that purported to be revelatory and were modeled on biblical writings. A fair number of these have survived, partly because they were accorded at least semiscriptural status by one group or another in the early centuries A.D. They are called respectively the Apocrypha ("obscure works") and the Pseudepigrapha ("works falsely attributed to a given author"). Though almost exclusively post-Old Testament in date, and though rejected from canonicity by Jewish and Christian councils (with the notable exception of the sixteenth-century Catholic formalization of the Apocrypha as canonical), these books are very closely related to parts of the OT and very useful to OT exegesis. Though neither inspired nor doctrinally reliable, they are useful for philological, topical, historical, and stylistic comparisons. In the sense of genre, they are "biblical" in their type, and thus suitable for comparative purposes. Whenever possible, therefore, you should pay attention to these noncanonical writings for the data they contain.

The classic publication of the Apocrypha and Pseudepigrapha was that of Charles:

> R. H. Charles (ed.), *The Apocrypha and Pseudepigrapha of the Old Testament: Vol. I, Apocrypha; Vol. 2, Pseudepigrapha* (Clarendon Press, 1913)

The best English translation of the pseudepigraphic books is now to be found in:

> James H. Charlesworth (ed.), *The Old Testament Pseudepigrapha*, 2 vols. (Doubleday, 1986)

Each of the fifty-three texts translated is given a brief introduction and some helpful critical notes. For information on NT apocryphal and pseudepigraphic literature, see:

James H. Charlesworth and James R. Mueller (eds.), *New Testament Apocrypha and Pseudepigrapha: A Guide to Publications, with Excurses on Apocalypses* (Scarecrow Press, 1987)

A good coverage of works on apocrypha and pseudepigrapha is available via the bibliography (pp. 113–22) in:

Joseph A. Fitzmyer, *An Introductory Bibliography for the Study of Scripture*, 3d ed. (Loyola Press, 1990)

An introduction to Apocrypha and Pseudepigrapha that also addresses other works is found in:

Leonhard Rost, *Judaism Outside the Hebrew Canon* (Abingdon Press, 1976)

On the Apocrypha, see also:

Bruce M. Metzger, *An Introduction to the Apocrypha* (Oxford University Press, 1977)

For analysis of how the OT pseudepigraphs relate to the NT, there is:

James H. Charlesworth, *The Old Testament Pseudepigrapha and the New Testament: Prolegomena for the Study of Christian Origins* (Trinity Press, 1998)

Also helpful are:

James H. Charlesworth, P. Dykers, and M. J. H. Charlesworth, *The Pseudepigrapha and Modern Research* (Scholars Press, 1981)
Mitchell G. Reddish (ed.), *Apocalyptic Literature: A Reader* (Hendrickson, 1996)

9.5. The Old Testament in the New

A demanding task is the analysis of OT themes, doctrines, etc., as they are reflected in the NT. All too often, OT exegetes neglect the NT data on the grounds that these represent later interpretations, muddying the exegetical waters. Unless you would go so far as to reject NT inspiration and authority, however, you are bound in the final analysis to relate the OT passage to any NT uses or classifications of it. As a general introduction to the principles involved, see:

F. F. Bruce, *The New Testament Development of Old Testament Themes* (Wm. B. Eerdmans, 1969)

Gregory K. Beale (ed.), *The Right Doctrine from the Wrong Texts? Essays on the Use of the Old Testament in the New* (Baker Book House, 1994)

Long out of print, but nevertheless the seminal work in the field, is:

C. H. Dodd, *According to the Scriptures: The Sub-structure of New Testament Theology* (Charles Scribner's Sons, 1953)

For a comprehensive list of NT citations and allusions to OT passages, consult the "Index of Quotations" (called in some editions "Index of Citations and Allusions") at the back of the latest edition of either the Nestle-Aland or the American Bible Society edition of the Greek New Testament.

10. Theology

10.1. Old Testament theologies

Because the major OT theologies attempt a broad coverage of books and passages, it is often possible to use them profitably for exegetical guidance in relating a passage to OT theology as a whole. However, a great diversity of outlook is represented by the various theologies, so they must be used with great caution. Some theologies reflect a perspective that downplays the significance or trustworthiness of given portions and passages of the OT in favor of others. Others respect carefully the univocality of the Scriptures. Nevertheless, a recognition of their biases does not mean that the theologies cannot be profitably used. In fact, if your own passage is slighted by the OT theologies or its issues are in your opinion ignored by them, it becomes precisely your responsibility—and opportunity—to demonstrate whether or not the theologies are derelict in doing so. If the theologies are found wanting, the force of your observations exegetically may be all the more significant and informative.

The theologies listed here are of varying dates. There is not much opportunity for theological concepts to go out of date, so one should not assume that the more recent works are automatically more valuable than the older ones. In general, it would be wise to consult as many of these as possible in preparing a thorough exegesis, because theologies differ from one another relatively more than other types of exegetical aids do.

Bruce C. Birch, Walter Brueggemann, and David L. Peterson, *A Theological Introduction to the Old Testament* (Abingdon Press, 1999)

Walter Brueggemann, *Theology of the Old Testament* (Fortress Press, 1997)

Walther Eichrodt, *Theology of the Old Testament*, 2 vols.; The Old Testament Library (Westminster Press, 1961, 1967)

Gerhard Hasel, *Old Testament Theology*, rev. ed. (Wm. B. Eerdmans, 1975)

Paul R. House, *Old Testament Theology* (Intervarsity Press, 1998)

Edmond Jacob, *Theology of the Old Testament* (Harper & Brothers, 1958)

Walter Kaiser, Jr., *Toward an Old Testament Theology* (Zondervan Publishing House, 1978)

James Muilenburg, *The Way of Israel: Biblical Faith and Ethics* (Harper & Row, 1961)

Horst Dietrich Preuss, *Old Testament Theology*, 2 vols. (Westminster John Knox Press, 1999)

Gerhard von Rad, *Old Testament Theology*, 2 vols. (Harper & Row, 1962, 1965)

John H. Sailhamer, *Introduction to Old Testament Theology: A Canonical Approach* (Zondervan Publishing House, 1995)

Ralph L. Smith, *Old Testament Theology: Its History, Method and Message* (Broadman and Holman, 1994)

Walther Zimmerli, *Old Testament Theology in Outline* (John Knox Press, 1978)

10.2. Christian theologies

Obviously, a Christian theology will give substantial attention to issues beyond the OT and will address some of the OT data less directly than will an OT theology. This broader perspective is valid and necessary for an exegesis to be entirely balanced in its conclusions. A most important criterion for exegetical value in a Christian theology is that it be biblically based, in constant dialogue with the text. In addition to the famous major theologies of well-known theologians such as Barth and Brunner, several works stand out as keenly biblical in orientation. The following each have various features to commend them to the exegete, and, again, it must be said that Christian theologies do not easily go out of date.

Herman Bavinck, *Our Reasonable Faith* (Wm. B. Eerdmans, 1956; repr. Baker Book House, 1977)

G. C. Berkouwer, *Studies in Dogmatics*, 14 vols. (Wm. B. Eerdmans, 1952–1976)

Donald Bloesch, *Christian Foundations*, 4 vols. (Intervarsity Press, 1992–2000)

Charles W. Carter (gen. ed.), *A Contemporary Wesleyan Theology*, 2 vols. (Zondervan Publishing House, 1984)

Millard J. Erickson, *Christian Theology*, 2d ed. (Baker Book House, 1998)

Wayne Grudem, *Systematic Theology: An Introduction to Biblical Doctrine* (Zondervan Publishing House, 2000)

Carl F. H. Henry, *God, Revelation and Authority*, 6 vols. (Word Books, 1976–1983)

Wolfhart Pannenberg, *Systematic Theology*, 3 vols. (Wm. B. Eerdmans, 1991)

Helmut Thielicke, *The Evangelical Faith*, 3 vols. (Wm. B. Eerdmans, 1974–1979)

Geerhardus Vos, *Biblical Theology* (Wm. B. Eerdmans, 1948)

Otto Weber, *Foundations of Dogmatics*, 2 vols. (Wm. B. Eerdmans, 1983)

H. Orton Wiley, *Christian Theology*, 3 vols. (Beacon Hill Press, 1940)

11. Secondary Literature

11.1. Special reference sources

Large numbers of valuable articles and books are published every year in the OT field. What if someone, somewhere, may once have written an article or a portion of a book dealing exegetically with your passage? It would be deplorable to ignore such a work if it could be readily attained. Especially if your exegesis is intended as a term paper or other substantial assignment, you could hardly afford not to consult a scholarly work devoted specifically to your topic.

For fast access to most of the significant books and journal articles written on your passage between 1930 and 1983, you can turn to one source that groups them all conveniently so that you don't have to make a year-by-year search for them:

Paul-Emile Langevin, *Bibliographie biblique, Biblical Bibliography, Biblische Bibliographie, Bibliografia biblica, Bibliografía biblica,* I (1930–1970);

II (1930–1975); III (1975–1983) (Quebec: L'Université Laval, 1972, 1978)

Volume I contains references only to Roman Catholic periodicals and books. Volume II adds non–Roman Catholic references, and brings the Roman Catholic references five years further along (1971–1975). Volume III brings both up to 1983.

A listing and an abstract (a brief summary) of virtually any recent book or article published on an OT topic can be found in *OTA*. Since 1978 the journal *Old Testament Abstracts* has provided brief summaries of the contents of nearly all significant articles and books written on OT studies year by year. From the abstracts you can get a sense of whether an article or book might be relevant to your study before investing the energy of hunting up the full publication itself. The articles are listed by category, and there are Scripture indexes, author indexes, and key (Hebrew / Aramaic) word indexes added. The *OTA* is so comprehensive that it has almost everything you will likely need after 1978. Consider subscribing. The address is:

> *Old Testament Abstracts*, Catholic Biblical Association of America, c/o The Catholic University of America, Washington, DC 20064.

OTA is also now available as computer software, allowing searches for individual Scripture references, key words in any language, authors, etc. You can even limit your search to works in English if you cannot read other languages. This is by far the best format of *OTA* for computer-literate exegetes.

From 1920 to 1930 all significant OT publications were tabulated yearly and listed both by topic and by Scripture reference in each annual addition of:

> *Elenchus Bibliographicus Biblicus*, vols. 1–48 (1920–1967) in the journal *Biblica*; published separately, 1968– (Vol. 49–)

For works published after 1930, Langevin and *Old Testament Abstracts* provide the same information, in easier-to-use formats.

The *Book List of the British Society for Old Testament Study* is an annual publication listing OT books produced each year since 1946. Its special value is that each book is given a mini-review, by which you can gauge something of its potential for your own research. The *Book List* listings have also been published in collections as follows:

> H. H. Rowley (ed.), *Eleven Years of Bible Bibliography* (1946–1956); (Falcon's Wing Press, 1957)
>
> G. W. Anderson (ed.), *A Decade of Bible Bibliography* (1957–1966); (Basil Blackwell, Publisher, 1967)
>
> P. R. Ackroyd (ed.), *Bible Bibliography 1967–1973: Old Testament* (Basil Blackwell, Publisher, 1974)
>
> Lester L. Grabbe (ed.), *Society for Old Testament Study Book List 1998* (Sheffield Academic Press, 1998)

The Institute for Biblical Research (IBR) publishes special bibliographies on various OT topics, and they are valuable for providing judicious listings of works in a given area. Notable examples include:

> Ewin C. Hostetter, *Old Testament Introduction*, IBR Bibliographies 11 (Baker Book House, 1995)
>
> Elmer A Martens, *Old Testament Theology*, IBR Bibliographies 13 (Baker Book House, 1997)
>
> Peter Enns, *Poetry and Wisdom*, IBR Bibliographies 3 (Baker Book House, 1997)

Since most readers of this book will have modern language proficiency mainly in English, the following series is of special note: A very fine listing of OT articles (grouped in 1,157 sections!) written in English since 1769 has been gathered in eight volumes within the excellent *ATLA Bibliography* series. The latest volume in the series covers articles written from 1987 to 1999:

> William G. Hupper (ed.), *An Index to English Periodical Literature of the Old Testament and Ancient Near East*, vol. 8 (Scarecrow Press, 1999)

11.2. The journals

Dozens of periodicals regularly carry articles related generally to the OT and specifically to OT exegesis. At the risk of slighting some of the best, a selection of ten journals is here recommended for their special attention to exegesis and exegetically important issues. The ten would likely be carried by most seminary libraries, and by many college and university libraries as well. If you make it a habit to pay attention to these journals, you will be rewarded by exposure to a steady flow of high-level exegetical content. All contain articles in English; most are written exclusively in English. The journals in alphabetical order are:

Biblica
Catholic Biblical Quarterly
Expository Times
Interpretation
Journal for the Study of the Old Testament
Journal of Biblical Literature
Revue Biblique
Vetus Testamentum
Westminster Theological Journal
Zeitschrift für die alttestamentliche Wissenschaft

11.3. Old Testament introductions

The various one-volume introductions to the OT provide the fastest means of access to a discussion of significant critical (exegetically oriented) points related to an OT book. In addition to Eissfeldt's classic *The Old Testament: An Introduction* (4.1.2), several other books are excellent and likely to be of substantial value if consulted in this manner. The following list represents some of the best works available in English:

Bernhard W. Anderson and Katheryn Pfisterer Darr, *Understanding the Old Testament, Abridged and Updated* (Prentice-Hall, 1997)

Gleason Archer, Jr., *A Survey of Old Testament Introduction*, rev. ed. (Moody Press, 1973)

Brevard S. Childs, *Introduction to the Old Testament as Scripture* (Fortress Press, 1979)

Raymond B. Dillard and Tremper Longman, III, *An Introduction to the Old Testament* (Zondervan Publishing House, 1994)

Georg Fohrer, *Introduction to the Old Testament* (Abingdon Press, 1968)

Norman K. Gottwald, *A Light to the Nations: An Introduction to the Old Testament* (Harper & Brothers, 1959)

Roland Kenneth Harrison, *Introduction to the Old Testament*, repr. (Prince Press, 1999)

Andrew E. Hill and John H. Walton, *A Survey of the Old Testament* (Zondervan Publishing House, 2000)

Paul R. House, *Old Testament Survey* (Broadman and Holman, 1994)

Otto Kaiser, *Introduction to the Old Testament* (Augsburg Publishing House, 1975)

William S. LaSor, David A. Hubbard, and Frederic W. Bush, *Old Testament Survey: The Message, Form and Background of the Old Testament* (Wm. B. Eerdmans, 1996)

J. Alberto Soggin, *Introduction to the Old Testament*, rev. ed.; The Old Testament Library (Westminster Press, 1982)

Edward J. Young, *An Introduction to the Old Testament*, rev. ed. (Wm. B. Eerdmans, 1958)

11.4. Commentaries

Of the dozens of commentary series, certain sets stand out as especially exegetical in format and interest. Commentary series are not consistent; you must actually evaluate each volume on its own merits. Works that do provide a book-by-book listing of commentaries include:

Douglas Stuart, *A Guide to Selecting and Using Bible Commentaries* (Word Books, 1987)

Brevard S. Childs, *Old Testament Books for Pastor and Teacher* (Westminster Press, 1977)

Tremper Longman, III, *Old Testament Commentary Survey* (Baker Book House, 1995)

A recent complete multivolume set is:

Frank E. Gaebelein (ed.), *The Expositor's Bible Commentary* [OT 7-vol. set] (Zondervan Publishing House, 1993); now also on CD–ROM

Some older major commentary series are still of tremendous value:

Carl Friedrich Keil and Franz Delitzsch, *A Commentary on the Old Testament*, 10 vols., repr. (Wm. B. Eerdmans, 1975)

International Critical Commentary on the Holy Scriptures (Charles Scribner's Sons, 1896–1951)

The Interpreter's Bible, 12 vols. (Abingdon Press, 1951–1957)

Of the several fine one-volume Bible commentaries, two may be mentioned as especially useful:

D. A. Carson, et al. (eds.), *The New Bible Commentary: Twenty-first Century Edition* (Intervarsity Press, 1994)

Raymond E. Brown, et al. (eds.), *The New Jerome Biblical Commentary* (Prentice-Hall, 1989)

The best, most recent exegetically oriented commentary series are all as yet incomplete. Notable are:

The Anchor Bible (Doubleday, 1946–) [also on CD-ROM]
Hermeneia (Fortress Press, 1971–)
The New International Commentary on the Old Testament (Wm. B. Eerdmans, 1955–). [almost complete; some works being rewritten]
The Old Testament Library (Westminster Press, 1961–)
The Word Biblical Commentary (Word Books, 1982–). [almost complete; also on CD–ROM]

Of these, the *Hermeneia* and *The Word Biblical Commentary* are the most technically exegetical. The ability to search the CD–ROM version of the *WBC* and *ABD* is certainly an advantage.

11.5. Bible dictionaries and Bible encyclopedias

A note on nomenclature: The term "Bible encyclopedia" is almost always applied to a multivolume sourcebook with thousands of entries (individual articles on topics). However, the term "Bible dictionary" can be used to indicate anything from a relatively small, single-volume dictionary with a few hundred entries to the most massive of all Bible dictionaries or encyclopedias, i.e., the *Anchor Bible Dictionary*.

A superb source of both comprehensive overview articles relating to theology and exegesis, as well as specific articles on individual Old Testament topics, is the *NIDOTTE*:

Willem A. VanGemeren (gen. ed.), *New International Dictionary of Old Testament Theology and Exegesis* (Zondervan Publishing House, 1998), 5 vols., now also on CD–ROM (2001)

The most comprehensive Bible dictionary is the *ABD*:

David Noel Freedman (ed.), *The Anchor Bible Dictionary*, 6 vols. (Doubleday, 1992)

Still the best for many topics and remarkable for its consistency of quality is the fully revised:

> G. W. Bromiley (gen. ed.), *The International Standard Bible Encyclopedia*, 4 vols. (Wm. B. Eerdmans, 1979–1988)

Still very useful, though aging, is:

> George A. Buttrick (ed.), *The Interpreter's Dictionary of the Bible*, 4 vols. (Abingdon Press, 1962)

To this a one-volume supplement was added:

> Keith Crim (ed.), *The Interpreter's Dictionary of the Bible, Supplementary Volume* (Abingdon Press, 1976)

Also excellent, and independently valuable for its conservative point of view on many exegetical issues, is:

> Merrill C. Tenney (gen. ed.), *The Zondervan Pictorial Encyclopedia of the Bible*, 5 vols. (Zondervan Publishing House, 1975)

A number of good one-volume Bible dictionaries are available. It might be thought that these would have little usefulness in light of the massive scale of giants like the *Anchor Bible Dictionary*. But, in fact, the size of the giants makes the one-volume dictionaries particularly valuable—for gaining a judicious overview or digest of the salient information on a topic. The articles in the huge multivolume sets, while prized for their thoroughness, can be so long as to leave the reader wondering what the most important facts really are. The articles in the smaller dictionaries often have the advantage of focus and true summative evaluation of the data by seasoned scholars.

An excellent example of the one-volume dictionaries is:

> I. Howard Marshall, et al. (eds.), *The New Bible Dictionary*, 3d ed. (Intervarsity Press, 1996)

The text of an earlier edition of the *NBD* was also published with a huge array of superb maps, charts, tables, and pictures as:

> *The Illustrated Bible Dictionary*, 3 vols. (Tyndale House, 1980)

Also of high quality is:

> J. D. Douglas, et al. (eds.), *The New International Bible Dictionary* (Zondervan Publishing House, 1999)

11.6. Other aids

A most welcome series of academic aids has been published by Fortress Press. These include some of the titles mentioned elsewhere in this primer. They explain in a readable, concise format such techniques as textual criticism, form criticism, literary criticism (including source criticism), sociological analysis, structural analysis, archaeology, and poetry criticism. The series is:

Guides to Biblical Scholarship: Old Testament Series (Fortress Press, 1971–)

Two major collections of illustrations relating to OT studies, each with thorough indexes, are often of value to the exegete. If you are analyzing a passage that mentions a site, a coin, a weight, an animal, a piece of furniture, a utensil, a weapon, or any place or object that might just "come alive" if illustrated, check these volumes to see if such an illustration might exist:

James B. Pritchard (ed.), The Ancient Near East in Pictures Relating to the Old Testament (Princeton University Press, 1954)

Some of the same illustrations are contained in a selection and combination of pictures from the above and texts from Pritchard's Ancient Near Eastern Texts Relating to the Old Testament (see 4.4.1):

James B. Pritchard (ed.), The Ancient Near East: An Anthology of Texts and Pictures (Princeton University Press, 1958)

This has been added to by:

James B. Pritchard (ed.), The Ancient Near East: Supplementary Texts and Pictures Relating to the Old Testament (Princeton University Press, 1969)

A second major collection is:

Clifford M. Jones, Old Testament Illustrations (Cambridge University Press, 1971)

On the area of the Dead Sea Scrolls, a most useful publication remains:

Joseph A. Fitzmyer, *The Dead Sea Scrolls: Major Publications and Tools for Study,* rev. ed. (Society of Biblical Literature and Scholars Press, 1990)

Fitzmyer introduces the various texts, explains where they and their translations are published, and outlines the contents of some of the major scrolls. He also provides an excellent bibliography and an index to biblical passages in the scrolls.

A good translation of the major Dead Sea Scrolls is found in:

Florentino García Martínez and Eibert J. C. Tigchelaar, *The Dead Sea Scrolls Translated: The Qumran Texts in English*, 2 vols. (Wm. B. Eerdmans, 1996)

Theodor H. Gaster, *The Dead Sea Scriptures: In English Translation with Introduction and Notes*, 3d ed. rev. and enl. (Doubleday, Anchor Books, 1976)

For definitions of terminology used in biblical studies, an alternative to Soulen's *Handbook* (see Introduction), though not as thorough, would be:

F. B. Huey, Jr., and Bruce Corley, *A Student's Dictionary for Biblical and Theological Studies* (Zondervan Publishing House, 1983)

Finally, when you need guidance to older bibliographic resources more broadly within the general field of theological study (church history, systematic theology, practical theology, missions, etc.—including biblical studies), consider:

John A. Bollier, *The Literature of Theology: A Guide for Students and Pastors* (Westminster Press, 1979)

11.7. Computer Bibles

Most of the "computer Bibles" are increasingly making available searchable resources that once were available only in book form. This is a very rapidly expanding area, and there can be little doubt that it will continue to expand. Fortunately, a lot of people who have a computer also have Internet access, and can either figure out how to locate the Web pages of the appropriate software publishers or know someone who can. The following is a limited sample of some of the more interesting, or valuable, or unique software modules available from software publishers. Some are deceptively titled (e.g., Bible Works is really an extensive package of different resources). The reader is advised to check out the full descriptions provided by the publishers at their Web sites, and to expect an ever-changing stream of additions and updates via the Web sites.

Oak Tree Software (www.oaksoft.com): AcCordance and Gramcord; *The AcCordance Bible Atlas; The Anchor Bible Dictionary*

Hermeneutika (www.bibleworks.com): BibleWorks

Logos Systems (www.logos.com): OT Hebrew Core Collection; NT Greek Core Collection; Scholar's Library; *Anchor Bible Dictionary; Logos Bible Atlas; The Dead Sea Scrolls Revealed; Kittel's Theological Dictionary of the New Testament*

Baker Digital Reference Library (www.bakerbooks.com): *Anchor Bible Dictionary; Word Biblical Commentary*; Koehler-Baumgartner, *Lexicon*; abridged Brown-Driver-Briggs *Lexicon; Biblical Archaeologist*, vols. 40–55; *Journal of the Evangelical Theological Society* (1969–present); *Westminster Theological Journal* (1970–present); *Biblioteca Sacra* (1934–present)

Silver Mountain Software (www.silvermt.com): Bible Windows

Zondervan (www.zondervan.com): *NIV Study Bible Complete Library; New International Dictionary of Old Testament Theology; New International Dictionary of New Testament Theology; Expositor's Bible Commentary*

Ages Software (www. ageslibrary.com): The Master Christian Library

Parsons Technology (www.parsonstech.com): Hebrew Tutor; Greek Tutor

Abingdon (www.abingdon.com): *The Interpreter's Bible; The Interpreter's Dictionary of the Bible*

Oxford (www.oup-usa.org): *The New Oxford Bible Maps; The New Oxford Annotated Biblical Reference Library; The Oxford Companion to the Bible*

Brill (www.brill.nl): *The Hebrew and Aramaic Lexicon of the Old Testament*, vols. 1–4

Phoenix Data Systems (www.phoenixdatasystems.com): Holy Land Explorer

Nelson Electronic Publishing (www.thomasnelson.com): *Word Biblical Commentary*

Paulist Press (www.paulistpress.com): *Old Testament Parallels*

Carta (www.science.co.il): *Carta's Comprehensive Bible Atlas*

Judaica Multimedia (www. judaica.com): *Encyclopedia Judaica*

Ellis Enterprises (www.biblelibrary.com): The Bible Library

Center for the Computer Analysis of Texts (www.ccat.sas.upenn.edu): Computer Assisted Tools for Septuagint Study; links to electronic resources, papyrus document resources, Christian origins resources

12. Application

12.1. Hermeneutics

Hermeneutics is the theory of understanding a passage's meaning. At virtually every stage of an exegesis, you are using hermeneutical (interpretational) principles, whether implicitly or explicitly. At the application stage, however, it is most important of all to be absolutely clear about the interpretational principles you employ since a proper application depends so greatly on reasonable and honest use of good principles. In other words, the rules you go by to interpret the passage will largely determine how accurately you apply the passage.

Traditionally—and simplistically—four different kinds of meanings have been discovered in biblical passages: (1) the literal (historical) meaning; (2) the allegorical (mystical or "spiritual") meaning; (3) the anagogic (typological—especially as relating to the end times and eternity) meaning; and (4) the tropological (moral) meaning. Precisely because the literal meaning was understood so narrowly (as merely the meaning the passage once had, rather than what it may also mean now), interpreters were driven to seek something personal, contemporary, and practical from the latter three types of meaning. After all, we read the Bible for help in our own lives, not just as a historical exercise. The latter types of meaning (allegorical, anagogic, tropological), however, are not usually directly derived from the passage itself, but tend to be more or less invented by the imagination according to rules not always consistently applied. Such kinds of interpretations are often seductively appealing, and can allow otherwise "dull" passages to seem to speak personally and practically. However, they usually ignore the intentionality of the text itself, so that what the ancient inspired author intended to be understood from his or her writing is grossly exceeded, indeed, eclipsed by almost uncontrolled mystical, typological, and moralizing sorts of overinterpretation.

The delicate task of the interpreter, then, is to be sure that everything the passage means is brought out but that nothing additional is read into the passage. We don't want to miss anything, but we don't want to "find" anything that isn't really there, either. Hermeneutics properly applied is thus interested in the boundaries of interpretation—the upper and lower limits—which are intended by the Spirit of God for the reader.

The most popular introduction to hermeneutics is the relatively brief and easy-to-read:

Gordon D. Fee and Douglas Stuart, *How to Read the Bible for All Its Worth*, 2d ed. (Zondervan Publishing House, 1993)

Hundreds of substantial volumes have been written on hermeneutics, most of them offering at least some helpful methodology. An excellent introduction to the theoretical issues is:

Kevin J. Vanhoozer, *Is There a Meaning in This Text?: The Bible, the Reader, and the Morality of Literary Knowledge* (Zondervan Publishing House, 1998)

The following are certainly among the best substantial works on hermeneutics, partly because they take seriously the authority and inspiration of the entire Bible:

Robert L. Hubbard, Jr., Craig L. Blomberg, William Klein, and Kermit L. Eckelbarger, *Introduction to Biblical Interpretation* (Word Publishing, 1993)

Anthony C. Thistleton, *New Horizons in Hermeneutics* (Zondervan Publishing House, 1992)

A. Berkeley Mickelsen, *Interpreting the Bible* (Wm. B. Eerdmans, 1963)

Grant R. Osborne, *The Hermeneutical Spiral: A Comprehensive Introduction to Biblical Interpretation* (Intervarsity Press, 1997)

Walter C. Kaiser, Jr., and Moisés Silva, *An Introduction to Biblical Hermeneutics: The Search for Meaning* (Zondervan Publishing House, 1994)

Roger Lundin, Anthony C. Thiselton, and Clarence Walhout, *The Promise of Hermeneutics* (William B. Eerdmans, 1999)

Roy B. Zuck (ed.), *Rightly Divided: Readings in Biblical Hermeneutics* (Kregel Publications, 1996)

D. Brent Sandy and Ronald L.Giese, *Cracking Old Testament Codes* (Broadman and Holman, 1995)

See also the following reference works on hermeneutics:

David S. Dockery, Robert B. Sloan, and Kenneth A. Matthews, *Foundations for Biblical Interpretation: A Complete Library of Tools and Resources* (Broadman and Holman, 1999)

John H. Hayes (ed.), *Dictionary of Biblical Interpretation*, 2 vols. (Abingdon Press, 1998)

In addition, a number of recent works on the hermeneutical task as it applies to preaching may be cited as particularly useful in their respective categories.

Practical encouragement toward the responsible extraction from a text of those features that will bring to a congregation a real sense of involvement with the "original" audience of scriptural events can be found in any of the following:

Wayne E. Ward, *The Word Comes Alive* (Broadman Press, 1969)

Haddon W. Robinson, *Biblical Preaching: The Development and Delivery of Expository Messages* (Baker Book House, 1980)

George L. Klein (ed.), *Reclaiming the Prophetic Mantle: Preaching the Old Testament Faithfully* (Broadman Press, 1992)

Two insightful books on many aspects of OT preaching have been penned by Elizabeth Achtemeier:

Elizabeth Achtemeier, *Preaching from the Old Testament* (Westminster John Knox Press, 1989)

Elizabeth Achtemeier, *Preaching Hard Texts of the Old Testament* (Hendrickson, 1998)

Either of the following should also prove helpful to you. Both have been standards in the field:

James W. Cox, *A Guide to Biblical Preaching* (Abingdon Press, 1976)

James W. Cox, *Preaching* (Harper and Row, 1985)

12.2. Some do's and don'ts in application

1.   Do consider the needs and composition of your audience in the way that you construct the application.

2. Do be careful that the application derives directly and logically from the passage (in other words, respect the passage's intentionality).

3. Do try to limit yourself if possible to the central or priority application.

4. Do—if your passage functions primarily to illustrate a principle stated elsewhere in Scripture—be sure to demonstrate a genuine relationship between the two.

1. Don't multiply applications needlessly (more is not necessarily better).

2. Don't assume that your audience will automatically make a proper application of the passage just because the rest of your exegesis is good.

3. Don't invent an application if none seems forthcoming. Better to say nothing rather than something misleading.

4. Don't confuse illumination with inspiration. The former refers to what you alone, emotionally, existentially, and individually may derive from the passage. The latter refers to what God has intended that the passage say to any of us in general. For illumination you should diligently appropriate for yourself a most precious, life-sustaining resource of the student and pastor, for which exegesis could never hope to substitute—prayer.

INDEX OF AUTHORS

Index of Scripture Passages

A List of Common
Old Testament
Exegesis Terms

antithetical: Describing poetic parallelism characterized by the pairing of an assertion and its contrast.

acrostic: Composed alphabetically, successive verses beginning with successive Hebrew letters (some psalms, sections of Proverbs, Lamentations, etc.).

anacolouthon: Grammatical non sequitur in which the first part of a thought is not completed as expected.

Aquila: Translated Hebrew Bible into Greek literalistically ca. 140 A.D.; included in Hexapla; replaced parts of LXX.

Aramaism: Word or idiom used in Hebrew, supposedly Aramaic in origin, therefore late in date. (Almost all have proved Semitisms, not late, and therefore not properly used for dating OT books late.)

assimilation: Replacement of an original text reading by a reading from another document.

asyndeton: Absence of conjunctions or other linking/coordinating words. (The Lord is my shepherd; I shall not want.) The reader must figure out the relationship of the concepts expressed.

autograph: The original, first copy of a biblical book or portion.

bifid: Organized into two discrete parts. (Many OT books are bifid; their two parts are not early and late respectively, or the products of different authors. They are just convenient ways of organizing the material thematically.)

chiasm (also chiasmus, inverted parallelism, etc.): A pattern of words or concepts in which the first and last are similar, the second and next to last are similar, etc., making memorization easy (e.g., Isa. 6:10; Zech. 14; Matt. 9:14). The middle of a chiasm is not necessarily more important than any other part. Most short chiasms are just stylistic variations within synonymous parallelisms.

codex: An ancient manuscript in book (bound pages) form rather than scroll form.

collate: To compare manuscripts of a given text in order to reconstruct the original.

colon: A single verse unit of poetry. (Usually people mean "one line of a couplet or triplet" by colon, but not always.)

colophon: Title or other summary at the end or beginning of a unit of text. (10 x's in Gen.; Lev. 26:46; etc.)

conflation: Combining two variant readings, producing a reading not the same as either of them.

daughter translation: A translation of a translation, usually referring to a translation of the LXX into another language.

deuterograph: Secondary writing/rewriting. (1–2 Chronicles contains deuterographs of 1 Sam.—2 Kings; cf. Ps. 14 and 53; etc.)

dittography: Copy error repeating something accidentally.

doublet: A supposedly parallel narrative, allegedly resulting from retelling in oral tradition (e.g., Gen. 12; 20; 26).

formula: A set of words commonly used in a particular kind of context. ("Thus says the Lord" is a messenger formula.)

hapaxlegomenon: A word or term that occurs only once in the OT (often making its definition hard to pin down).

haplography: The loss of something during copying (letters, words, sentences, etc. that the copyist skips accidentally).

hendiadys: Expressing a single concept by two or more words or expressions linked by "and" (lord and master; arise and go). (In translating accurately you often have to eliminate or subordinate one of the words, e.g., lord; get going; etc.)

Hexapla: Origen's six-column OT containing (1) the Hebrew, (2) the Hebrew transliterated into Greek; (3) Aquila, (4) Symmachus, (5) the LXX, and (6) Theodotion. (The LXX he produced was highly conflated, with asterisks used to indicate what he had added to the original LXX and obeluses used to indicate what he had subtracted from it.)

homoioarchton: Similar beginnings in two words (thus causing the scribe accidentally to skip from the one to the other).

homoioteleuton: Similar endings in two words (thus causing the scribe accidentally to skip from the one to the other).

inclusio: Literary device in which the end and the beginning of a passage are similar, thus sandwiching the rest.

Kethib and Qere: Kethib = Inferior reading that the Masoretes included in the text by writing only its consonants. *Qere*: Superior reading that the Masoretes imposed over the *Kere* consonants by using only its vowels.

lacuna: A physical gap in a manuscript.

meter: The pattern of accents and/or total syllables in a passage of poetry. All musical poetry has meter.

metonymy: A word substitution (e.g., "juice" for electricity; "heaven" for God in Matt.; "crown" for Caesar in Rev. 13:3).

paleography: Study of ancient writing/penmanship. For example, the style of the letters can tell the age of a document.

parallelism: The logical balances and correspondences between lines of poetry (e.g., synonymous, antithetical, synthetic).

paronomasia: A pun or play on words or word roots (pleasing to the ear, aids memorization).

Peshitta: The most common Syriac version of the OT.

prostaxis: The tendency to start all the clauses in a language in the same way. Hebrew uses prostactic *we* ("and").

Qinah meter: Supposedly a three-accent + two-accent pattern used in dirges (a misunderstanding of the meter in Lamentations).

Rîb form: A literary form by which a nation is imagined taken to court, usually to be tried and found guilty.

Septuagint: Greek translation of the Hebrew OT originally made between about 200 and 100 B.C., modified often.

Symmachus: Independent, freestyle translation of the OT into Greek around 175 A.D.; influenced Vulgate.

synecdoche: A part used for the whole, or vice versa ("Nice threads!" "Got wheels?" "turning the world upside down").

synonymous: Describing poetic parallelism in which the same essential concept is conveyed by two different wordings that are parallel to each other.

synthetic: Describing poetic parallelism in which the first half of a complete assertion is paralleled and completed by the second half.

Talmud : Huge Jewish rabbinical teaching collection: Mishnah [traditions] and Gemara [commentary on Mishnah], 3d–5th cents. A.D.

Targum: Aramaic translation of the OT. There are various sections, produced at various times, probably 2d–5th cents. A.D.

terminus a quo: The earliest possible date for something.

terminus ad quem: The latest possible date for something.

Theodotion: Greek revision of the LXX toward the Hebrew, ca. 175 A.D.; replaced the old LXX in most Daniel MSS.

variant: A different reading (thus requiring the text critic to consider whether it represents the original or not).

Vulgate: Free translation of the OT into Latin by St. Jerome, completed 405 A.D. (replaced the older and often better Old Latin).

A LIST OF FREQUENT
HERMENEUTICAL ERRORS

Personalizing: Assuming that any or all parts of the Bible apply to you or your group in a way that they do not apply to everyone else. ("What Balaam's ass says to me is that I talk too much.") Also known as *individualizing.*

Universalizing: Assuming that something unique or uncommon in the Bible applies to everyone equally. ("We all have our Gethsemanes.") Also known as *generalizing.*

Spiritualizing: Assuming that events or factors have their real application in some religious truth beyond what they actually say. ("The lovely structure of the Jerusalem Temple encourages us to have our own lives well in order.")

Moralizing: Assuming that principles for living can be derived from all passages. ("We can learn much about parenting by noting how the father of the prodigal son handled his wayward child.") (The Egyptians drowned at the Red Sea because they had vacillated. You can't vacillate and expect to succeed in this life.")

Exemplarizing: Assuming that because someone in the Bible did something, it is an example for us to follow. ("To learn how to tell stories in sermons, let us examine Jesus' storytelling.") ("Let's see how Jesus called disciples and let that be the model for our evangelism.") ("What can we learn about adversity from how the Israelites endured their years as slaves in Egypt?")

Allegorizing: Assuming that the components of a passage have meaning only as symbols of Christian truths. ("The 'lover' is Christ; the 'beloved' is the Church; the 'daughters of Jerusalem' are the Scriptures.")

Typologizing: Assuming that certain real biblical characters or things are mentioned in order to foreshadow other real—and more important—characters or things. ("Joshua has the same name as Jesus; as a conqueror he points to The Conqueror.") ("Ezra came to his people from afar; entered into Jerusalem on a donkey; prayed before crises; taught what was to many a new law; purified the nation, etc. His life points directly to the Savior.")

The Root Fallacy: Assuming that the/an original meaning of a word always attends its usage. ("To be holy means to be set apart.") [cf. terrible/terrific/terrifying]

Genre confusion: Assuming that the interpretational rules for one genre apply to another. ("Jesus' parable of the workers in the vineyard contains seven helpful perspectives on the value of hard work.") ("The Twenty-third Psalm teaches us how to care for those under our authority.") ("According to Deuteronomy 33, if we trust God we'll never lack anything.") ("But Proverbs promises that if we honor God we'll be well liked by everyone!")

Totality transfer: Assuming that all the possible meanings of a word or phrase go with it whenever it is used. ("Head [*kephale*], of course, means 'source' here, just as it does in Xenophon's reference to the source of a river.")

Argument from silence: Assuming that everything relevant to an issue is mentioned in the Bible every time that issue is mentioned. ("Notice that Paul does not explicitly condemn premarital sex anywhere in his letters.")

Argument from authority: Assuming that the views of "experts" or a preponderance of them must be correct. ("Smith, who has devoted his life to studying Ruth, may be trusted . . .") ("Since this is held by few scholars, it does not seem tenable.")

Israel-Church confusion: Assuming that things that apply to biblical Israel also apply to the church. ("We can learn how to discipline troublesome kids from this law about stoning disobedient children.")

Israel-modern nation confusion: Assuming that things that apply to biblical Israel also apply to modern nations ("According to 2 Chronicles 7:14, if we pray and repent God will heal America.")

Israel-modern Israel confusion: Assuming that the modern, secular state named Israel in the Near East is the Israel referred to in the Bible. ("How can we support the Saudis when they're the enemies of God's chosen people?")

False combination: Joining two statements or passages in such a way as to produce a hybrid conclusion. ("In Matthew 25 Jesus calls hell both outer darkness and also fire, so hell fire must be some kind of special divine fire that doesn't give off any light. You can feel it but you can't see it.")

Figure of speech confusion: Failure to understand any of the many nonliteral expressions in human speech, especially metaphors. ("Imagine the massive scale of Canaanite dairy farming and beekeeping that led to Canaan's being called a land flowing with milk and honey.")

Equivocation: Confusing a term or concept with another term or concept, thus misunderstanding its meaning. ("1 Thessalonians 5 says to 'abstain from all appearance of evil' so you can't even ask directions from a prostitute.")

False presupposition: Basing all or part of an argument or conclusion on incorrect assumptions. ("The Hebrew mind thought concretely; the Greek mind abstractly. This is why the OT has more rituals and the NT more symbols.")